NATURE'S BOUNTY:
MORE ABOUT FOODS FOR A
LONGER AND HEALTHIER LIFE

Library of Congress Control Number: 2004118145

To order additional copies, please contact us.
BookSurge, LLC
www.booksurge.com
1-866-308-6235
orders@booksurge.com

DR. BALA NAIDOO

NATURE'S BOUNTY:
MORE ABOUT FOODS FOR A LONGER AND HEALTHI- ER LIFE

2005

NATURE'S BOUNTY:
MORE ABOUT FOODS FOR A
LONGER AND HEALTHIER LIFE

CONTENTS

FOREWORD

Following the many encouraging comments I received after the publication of my first book, "Nature's Bounty: Why Certain Foods Are So Good For You", published in the fall of 2004, I decided to embark on a second one in the same vein. The contents of "Nature's Bounty: More about Foods for a Longer and Healthier Life" are also drawn from a collection of articles written for the weekly community newspaper "Your Local Journal" and deal with the health benefits of certain types of food. The articles were written after doing a thorough research of the literature and include only studies done at reputable institutions around the world.

Nutrition has long been a major interest of mine, and in particular how the right kind of diet can help you live a longer and healthier life. I have been gratified to find that this interest is shared by many other people in the community.

I would like to thank all those who have made suggestions with regards to topics for my column and also for the many invitations I have received to talk about my first book and its contents.

I hope readers, especially those who want to know more about the food they eat, will derive as much benefit from reading my second book as they have from reading the first.

Dr. Bala Naidoo,
July 24, 2005

Please note that this book has been written to help you make informed decisions concerning your diet and your health. However, if you have a medical problem, please do not use the information in this book for self-treatment. It is not intended to replace medical advice given by a physician.

To my parents, especially my mother, who first taught me about good food and to Pauline, Robin, Loren and Sarah for all the good meals we have shared over the years.

I would like to thank my wife, Pauline McManus (former editor of Your Local Journal) for all her help and advice in putting this book together.

AVOCADOES: FRUITS OF PARADISE

I n this single delectable fruit are combined the protein of meat, the fat of butter, the vitamins and minerals of green vegetables, the flavor of nuts, a six course dinner." Quite an appropriate description of the nutritional value of avocadoes by Gaylord Hauser, the noted American food writer!

Avocadoes (*Persea Americana*) originated in Central and South America and then spread to the West Indies and the tropical areas of Asia, Africa and Australia. Today, there are many varieties of avocadoes depending on their origin— Mexican, Guatemalan or West Indian.

The two most common ones available here are the small, rough-skinned Haas from California and the larger, smooth-skinned Fuerte from Florida. At maturity, the skin of the Haas variety changes colour from green to dark purple while the Fuerte stays green. Avocadoes are ripe when the flesh gives on gentle squeezing. If they are hard, avocadoes can be ripened by keeping them in a sealed paper bag for a few days.

Avocadoes are an excellent source of potassium and vitamins such as A, B1, B6, E and folate. The Haas avocado has more nutrients, including minerals such as calcium, manganese, phosphorus and magnesium, and more fat than the Fuerte. In fact, a Haas avocado provides much of our daily nutritional needs.

Avocadoes are very versatile and can be used as a salad, an entrée, a soup, a dessert or a dip. After being cut, the flesh should not be left exposed to the air as it will turn brown.

Although avocadoes are high in fat, it is mostly oleic acid, a monounsaturated fatty acid similar to that found in olive oil, and is heart-healthy.

We need some fat in our diet for forming hormones and absorbing fat-soluble vitamins. However, we have to choose the right kind of fat, such as mono or polyunsaturated ones. A study showed that people with high cholesterol levels who added avocadoes to their regular diet for only one week had lower values of total cholesterol and 'bad' LDL cholesterol, together with higher 'good' HDL cholesterol.

As early as 1990, an epidemiological study done in Italy and published in The Journal of the American Medical Association found that, even though both monounsaturated and polyunsaturated fats lower cholesterol when compared to the saturated fats found in meat, cheese and butter, only monounsaturated fats lower blood pressure. Interestingly, it has been found that replacing saturated fat in the diet with mostly monounsaturated fats can also result in a small loss of weight and a lower risk of breast cancer.

Avocadoes are rich in potassium and low in sodium, in the ratio of 50:1; they can, therefore, help reduce high blood pressure and lower the risk of heart disease and stroke. Studies have shown that avocadoes and bananas have some of the highest levels of potassium among fruits and vegetables. Research done at the University of California at San Diego and at Cambridge University showed that increasing the potassium intake by about 400mg daily reduces the risk of a stroke by 40%. And did you know you can get that amount in half an avocado?

Avocadoes are also a good source of folate, with one cup providing a quarter of our daily requirement of this important, heart-friendly B vitamin. Another B vitamin they contain is B6 or pyridoxine, which is required for the health of the nervous system and red blood cells. In fact, avocadoes have one of the highest levels of vitamin B6 of all vegetables and fruits.

Studies done at Washington State University have shown that low levels of vitamin B6 in the diet can cause DNA strands to break, which could eventually lead to cancer. Another study done at the Harvard School of Public Health, and published in the Journal of the National Cancer Institute, found that of 30,000 women, those who had the highest blood level of vitamin B6 had a 30% reduced risk of breast cancer compared to those with the lowest levels.

Vitamin B6 forms part of several co-enzymes that are involved in building and breaking down biological compounds in the body, such as converting folate to thymine, which is one of the four chemicals that, when paired up, form DNA. So, if the level of vitamin B6 is low, another chemical, uracil, is sometimes substituted for thymine, leading to a compromised DNA.

The average requirement for vitamin B6 is slightly over one milligram per day but it is estimated that in North America most people do not get that amount. Besides avocadoes, other foods that are rich in vitamin B6 include bananas, legumes, meat and fish.

Avocadoes also contain antioxidants such as vitamins E and C and beta-carotene as well as the minerals copper and iron, which form part of antioxidant enzymes and may thus provide protection against heart disease, arthritis, eye diseases and cancer.

A University of Florida researcher reported in a 2004 issue of the Biological Research for Nursing that vitamin E and exercise may slow down the ageing process by neutralizing free radicals which can cause oxidative stress leading to diseases and ageing of the body. Almonds, vegetable oils, whole grains and spinach are other good sources of vitamin E.

Recent research carried out by Dr. H. Kawagishi at Shizuoka University in Japan has shown that when rats, whose livers were damaged by the liver toxin galactosamine, had avocadoes added to their diet for two weeks, the damage became less severe. Although further research is planned to see if a similar effect is found in humans, the good doctor has been eating more avocadoes himself and now recommends that we should try and eat one a day. Protection of the liver is important since it is the organ that detoxifies the body of toxic chemicals absorbed from the air, food, water and the environment.

Avocadoes contain relatively high amounts of both soluble and insoluble fibre. As the fibre intake of most people in the West is woefully inadequate, addition of avocadoes to the diet would be a pleasant way to make up for that deficit.

An oil can be extracted from avocadoes, which is not only used in cooking but also in cosmetics since it is safe, biodegradable and is well absorbed by the skin. It is even effective as a sunscreen.

By the way, the name avocado is derived from the Aztec word for testicle—which goes to show that the Aztecs had vivid imaginations!

CHERRIES: SWEET AND SOUR

Cherries are thought to have originated from Asia Minor, near the Caspian Sea. Today, two major species of cherries are grown commercially, sweet cherry (Prunus avium) and sour cherries (Prunus cerasus). Many cultivars were brought from Europe such as Hedelfingen or Black Tartarian but some were also developed in Canada, Vega and Stella being prime examples.

Sweet cherries include the Bing or Black Tartarian, which are deep burgundy, and the Royal Ann or Rainier, which are yellow with red blushes. When processed and dyed red, Royal Ann cherries are sold as Maraschino cherries for use in drinks and desserts. There are four kinds of sweet cherries: light- and dark-coloured Hearts and Bigarreaus. The Hearts have a soft flesh and the dark ones have red juices. The Bigarreaus have firmer flesh and are, therefore, widely grown commercially. Commonly grown sour cherries are the Montmorency and Morello.

The fruits, which are known as drupes or stone fruits, are eaten fresh, used in pies and preserves, or transformed into cherry cider and liqueurs. Small amounts of toxic compounds containing cyanide are found in the kernels of cherry stones, as well as in those of the related plums and apricots.

Both sweet and sour cherries contain antioxidants that are believed to help relieve pain by reducing inflammation. Sour cherries rank high on the ORAC (Oxygen Radical Absorption

Capacity) scale. Antioxidants such as anthocyanins, cyanidin, catechins, chlorogenic acid, flavonoids such as queritrin and isoqueritrin, and melatonin that are found in cherries, mop up free radicals which would otherwise damage cells and cause diseases. It has been shown that some of these antioxidants are as powerful as vitamin E or vitamin C in preventing the oxidation of LDL cholesterol, a first step in the formation of plaques in the arteries.

Scientists from Michigan State University showed, in a paper published in 2004 in the Journal of Natural Products, that the red pigments in sour cherries, anthocyanins and cyanidin, have antioxidant and anti-inflammatory activities, presumably by inhibiting COX-1 and COX-2 enzymes, just like aspirin, ibuprofen and other NSAID drugs. These drugs produce side effects such as upset stomachs, vomiting, kidney problems and stomach ulcers, which is not the case with cherries.

Not surprisingly there are anecdotal reports for the effectiveness of both sweet and sour cherries against arthritis, gout and migraine headaches.

It appears that high dietary levels of anthocyanins are needed in order to get the desired effect in the body since these pigments are not well absorbed. Eating 20 fresh cherries provides about 25 milligrams of anthocyanins, enough to stop enzymes causing inflammation, thus reducing the pain associated with arthritis and gout.

In a 2003 issue of the American Society for Nutritional Sciences Journal of Nutrition, scientists at the University of California at Davis found that women consuming 45 fresh, sweet Bing cherries had 15% less uric acid in their blood. Eating that number of cherries for three to 90 days brought the uric acid value to normal levels and reduced the pain associated with gout. High levels of uric acid cause crystals of monosodium urate to be formed in joints of the toes for example, which cause inflammation and pain.

Cherries also contain several compounds which have anticancer and antimutagenic properties, such as queritrin, isoqueritrin, ellagic acid and perillyl alcohol. According to studies at the University of Iowa, perillyl alcohol starves cancer cells of the proteins they need for their growth, thus reducing the risk of cancer by up to 50%. In animal studies, cancer regression occurred in 81% of small breast cancer and 75% of advanced breast cancer cases. This indicates that perillyl alcohol is about five times more potent than other known compounds that cause tumour regression.

Research done at the University of Texas Health Science Centre in San Antonio has found that cherries, especially sour cherries, are rich in melatonin, a hormone formed in the brain's pineal gland, which controls the body's circadian rhythms and sleep patterns and, through its antioxidant properties, could even prevent ageing. Montmorency cherries contain about 13.5 nanograms of melatonin per gram of cherries, more than is found in any other fruits. Being both water and fat-soluble, melatonin is a more potent antioxidant than either the water-soluble vitamin C or the fat-soluble vitamins A and E. Since ageing reduces the body's production of melatonin, which may cause sleep problems, eating sour cherries may be an inexpensive way of increasing levels of melatonin in older people.

According to a recent article in the Journal of Agricultural and Food Chemistry, chemicals in both sweet and sour cherries may help fight against type-2 diabetes by improving insulin sensitivity.

On a sweet note, Shakespeare's A Midsummer Night's Dream associates cherries with love and romance and, in fact, the cherry has been linked to virginity since ancient times, perhaps because the red fruit, with its enclosed seed, symbolizes the uterus!

CRANBERRIES: NOT JUST FOR THANKSGIVING AND CHRISTMAS!

Native to North America, cranberries (Vaccinium macrocarpon) belong to the same family as blueberries. They grow in conditions that would not support other crops i.e. acid soil, low nutrients and low temperatures. They are usually cultivated in sandy bogs and when the fruits are ready for harvest, the bogs are flooded and the floating fruits can then be easily collected.

Cranberries have been used for centuries as food and medicine by Native Americans. The most popular use was in the making of pemmican, a survival cake made of dried meat, crushed cranberries, cornmeal and fat. It was dried in the sun and, since it did not spoil, was used as food on long journeys. They also made bread with cornmeal mixed with crushed cranberries. The juice provided a refreshing drink thanks to its sour taste, which is due to the presence of organic acids such as citric, malic and benzoic acids.

Modern research is showing that cranberries may protect our health as a result of their antioxidant and anti-adhesion properties.

Cranberries are rich in antioxidants such as vitamin C, flavonoids, proanthocyanidins, anthocyanins, quercetin and tocotrienols. On the antioxidant scale, cranberries are right near the top according to scientists at the Agricultural Research Service of USDA and the University of Massachusetts-

Dartmouth. Of twenty common fruit juices tested, cranberry juice cocktail had the highest antioxidant level. This is measured using the Oxygen Radical Absorbance Capacity (ORAC) values, which reflect the ability to destroy free radicals. Antioxidants neutralize free radicals in the body which are linked to diseases such as cancer, heart disease and diabetes.

Cranberries contain flavonoids, polyphenols and other antioxidants that have been shown to inhibit 'bad' LDL cholesterol oxidation, a first step leading to atherosclerosis. In addition, the fruit is rich in fibre, especially pectin, which could also help lower cholesterol. In fact, human studies have shown that drinking three glasses of cranberry cocktail per day increases the 'good' HDL cholesterol level in blood, thus reducing the risk of getting heart disease.

Cranberries can improve the elasticity of our arteries. A recent study done at the University of Wisconsin-Madison showed that cranberries improved the ability of blood vessels to relax in pigs that have been bred to have high cholesterol.

Cranberries may also possess anticancer properties, according to studies done at the University of Illinois and the University of Western Ontario. Scientists have isolated several bioactive compounds from cranberries, which have been found to have anti-cancer properties against some tumour cell lines.

In studies carried out at the University of Wisconsin-Madison, cranberries were found to inhibit the growth of several common pathogens although they did not seem to affect the growth of good bacteria. In this respect, cranberries behaved like a probiotic, helping good bacteria but killing off bad ones.

Since cranberries are high on the antioxidant scale, they can protect against age-related afflictions such as loss of coordination and memory, which are thought to be caused by free radical damage. Experiments using animal models have shown that rats, whose diets are supplemented with cranberries, have more protection for their brain cells against free radical damage and subsequent loss of motor skills and cognitive function in old age.

Cranberry juice has long been used to treat urinary tract infections. It was originally thought that acidification of the urine by the juice was responsible for its antibacterial action. However, a 2002 article in the Journal of the American Medical Association identified proanthocyanidins in cranberries as being the active agents. They inhibit the adhesion of bacteria which is necessary for infection to flourish, in the lining of the urinary tract. An 8-ounce serving of cranberry cocktail was found to protect bladder cells from E. coli bacteria for up to 10 hours. So, two servings per day would offer complete protection against the disease. The antimicrobial effect of drinking cranberry juice daily for 6 months remains for a further 6 months, even if no extra juice is drunk.

The benefits of anti-adhesion may also extend to the mouth and the gastrointestinal tract. Research is singling out a high molecular weight constituent of cranberries for its ability to protect against peptic ulcers by preventing the adhesion of Helicobacter pylori bacteria to the stomach lining and gastric mucus. Similarly, the same component can limit the adhesion of Streptococcus mutans bacteria to one another and to gum surfaces, which gives rise to the dental plaque responsible for cavities and gum diseases. Some of these conditions, which would require the use of antibiotics, could conceivably be more safely treated with cranberry juice instead.

Cranberry juice is rich in oxalic acid although the level is not as high as was once believed. However, if you are prone to forming kidney stones, you should not overindulge in cranberry juice.

There is little risk of most people gorging on pemmican though! But don't judge frontier cooking solely on pemmican since cranberry sauce, made by sweetening cranberries with maple sugar or honey, was also invented at that time!

MELONS: SMALL OR BIG, THEY ARE GOOD FOR YOU

We remember the fish that we did eat in Egypt freely: the cucumbers, and the melons, and the leeks, and the onions, and the garlick" (Numbers 11:5).

Melons are thought to have originated in the Middle East, principally Iran and Egypt, as evidenced by an Egyptian tomb painting dated 2400B.C. They then spread to Europe and were brought to the New World by the early explorers. Melons are held in high esteem in many parts of the world and there is even a holiday, Muskmelon Day, in Turkmenistan to celebrate the melon.

Melons belong to the Cucurbitaceae family just like pumpkins, squash and cucumbers. They come in various sizes, shapes and colours, such as the white-fleshed Casaba melon, the orange-fleshed muskmelon and cantaloupe, the salmon-fleshed Crenshaw, the green-fleshed Honeydew melon and the canary melon with its bright yellow skin and white flesh. The cantaloupe, which is known as Charentais in France, and the muskmelon have a rough, netted pattern on the skin unlike other melons.

Melons with an orange-coloured flesh have high levels of beta-carotene, which is converted in the body to vitamin A. A cup of cantaloupe supplies almost all of our daily requirements in vitamin A. Honeydew melons, on the other hand, have very little beta-carotene but are the sweetest of all the melons.

Since they don't travel well when ripe, melons are picked when they are not quite ripe. Except for Casaba melons, which have no aroma, ripe melons sometimes can be detected by their aroma, and by the hollow sound they make when gently tapped. Since melons do not have excess starch, which could be converted to sugar, they do not get any sweeter after harvesting.

Most melons are not only rich in beta-carotene but also in vitamin C, fibre, potassium, calcium and iron. They have been found to help protect against many diseases.

For example, people who ate cantaloupes regularly had 50% less need for cataract surgery. Furthermore, in a study of 50,000 middle-aged nurses, those having the highest dietary intake of vitamin A had 39% less risk of getting cataracts.

The high levels of vitamin A in cantaloupes may protect against emphysema if you are a smoker. According to research carried out at Kansas State University, a deficiency of this vitamin can be caused by benzo(a)pyrene, a carcinogen commonly found in cigarette smoke. This can be counteracted by a diet containing plenty of foods rich in vitamin A, such as carrots and melons.

Cantaloupe should also be a part of your daily fruit intake since a large study carried out over more than a decade, published in the Archives of Opthalmology, has shown that eating three fruits per day reduced the risk of macular degeneration by 36% in older adults, compared to those who ate less. Surprisingly, consumption of vegetables or supplementing with vitamins A, C, E and carotenoids did not reduce the risk of getting this disease, which is the major cause of blindness in people over 65.

Cantaloupes and other melons also contain the water-soluble vitamin C as well as the fat-soluble vitamin A, both antioxidants that help protect against free radicals in aqueous and fat media respectively, thus reducing the risk of heart disease and cancer. Vitamin C also enhances the immune system and is therefore critical for good health. One cup of cantaloupe supplies much of the vitamin C we need per day. We need to eat food rich in vitamin C every day since, unlike vitamin A, any excess vitamin C is not stored but excreted in the urine.

Melons are also good sources of dietary fibre, several B vitamins such as B6, folate and B3, which are used for processing carbohydrates, and may therefore be beneficial for diabetics.

Before eating a melon, it should be washed with water containing some bleach, and then with clean water, to kill any bacteria that could adhere to the scaly skin and contaminate the flesh when it is cut. Numerous cases of Salmonella infections, as a result of consuming cantaloupes grown in Mexico, have been reported in the US. For example, an article in the Journal of Infectious Diseases in 1999 reported an outbreak of Salmonella infections in the US resulting from people eating Mexican-grown cantaloupes, without first washing them.

Cucurbitacins, the extremely bitter constituents found in unusually large quantities in some mutant melons, zucchinis and watermelons, are being investigated as substitutes for poisonous insecticides used at present to eradicate corn rootworms. Unlike other insects and mammals, which stay clear of these bitter-tasting compounds, rootworm beetles just love them because after eating them, their bodies become so bitter that insect-loving birds avoid them! Scientists, looking for rootworm poisons to add to cucurbitacins, are trying the photoactive red dye #28 which is already used in cosmetics. The dye, laced with melon juice, forms red dots on leaves which attract the rootworm beetles. After feeding on them, the beetles become red in colour and are killed, as a result of a photochemical reaction after five minutes exposure to sunlight. A bitter end indeed!

OLIVES: A MINE OF LIQUID GOLD!

For many people, the olive is a tasty snack or something you put on top of a pizza. What is inside this small fruit, though, makes it a more valuable addition to the diet.

The olive (Olea europaea) has been around for a long time. It is thought to have originated in Asia Minor. From there, it spread to Syria and, thanks to the Phoenicians, was first brought to the Greek islands and then to the mainland itself around the 12th century B.C. Towards the 6th century, olive trees were growing throughout the Mediterranean area, including southern Italy. The Romans introduced the plant throughout their empire, where the climate was suitable. The conquest of Spain by the Arabs led to the introduction of their own special varieties, which were so widely cultivated that, even today, the Spanish word for olive, aceituna, is derived from Arabic. Today, Italy, Spain and Greece are the main producers of olives.

Olives are green in colour when unripe and turn black when fully ripe. There are several popular varieties of green olives such as the Spanish manzanilla and French picholine. As for black varieties, Greek kalamata and Italian liguria or gaeta are top favourites.

Fresh olives are bitter and acrid due to the presence of a compound in the skin called oleuropin. To remove the bitterness, olives are soaked in water, brine or oil. Green olives have to be treated with a solution of sodium hydroxide first to soften them and then they can be pickled in salt water. Black olives do not have to go through the initial softening process but can be pickled in salt water right away after harvesting. The appearance and taste of each variety of olives depends on its ripeness at harvesting and on the pickling process that was used.

Ripe olives contain more oil than green ones. However, the best olive oil is obtained by blending oil from nearly ripe olives that have turned red, but not black, with some from green olives of a different variety. High quality oil with low acidity is obtained by cold pressing of the fruits, without any other additional treatment.

The best quality olive oil is the extra virgin oil, which varies from yellowish-green to bright green in colour and has an acidity level of 1%. Virgin olive oil is slightly more acidic with between 1 and 3% acidity. Next comes fino olive oil, which is a blend of the above two and last is light olive oil which, through refining, has lost much of its flavour. However, the latter can be used for cooking at high temperatures.

Don't be fooled by the label 'Pure Olive Oil' which is, in fact, a lower quality oil obtained by blending some extra virgin oil with refined olive oil. Olive oil should be kept tightly sealed and protected from heat and light since the latter will degrade it. Olive oil contains 75% of oleic acid, a monounsaturated fatty acid as well several vitamins, notably vitamin E, and many polyphenols.

As for the medical benefits of olive oil, which were first mentioned by Hippocrates, countries in the Mediterranean area where it is an important part of the diet have a lower incidence of heart disease and certain cancers. This has been attributed partly to oleic acid, which can reduce the 'bad' LDL cholesterol and increase the 'good' HDL cholesterol.

Polyunsaturated fatty acids such as those found in corn

(57%), sunflower (71%) or safflower (76%) oils reduce both LDL and HDL cholesterol. In a randomized study comparing these two types of fatty acids, it was found that people consuming olive oil had lower levels of total cholesterol and LDL cholesterol in their blood than those taking sunflower oil. However, it is likely that antioxidants, such as vitamin E and polyphenols, present in olive oil, especially the extra virgin oil from the first pressing, also play a role in this process. Indeed, it was found that polyphenols such as oleuropein and hydroxytyrosol, which are present in olive oil, inhibit oxidation of LDL cholesterol, a first step in plaque formation, which could lead to a heart attack. Furthermore, sunflower oil containing a similar amount of monounsaturated fatty acid as olive oil did not reduce cholesterol to the same extent as olive oil did, indicating that other compounds in it, most likely polyphenols, must be at work here.

Other studies have found that people who consumed two tablespoonfuls of virgin olive oil every day for a week had less LDL cholesterol oxidation and higher blood levels of polyphenols.

Olive oil is, of course, not the only dietary factor which helps lower 'bad' LDL cholesterol and increase 'good' HDL cholesterol. Recent research indicates that switching to a so-called Mediterranean diet can also be beneficial. That involves reducing consumption of red meat and dairy products and replacing other fats with olive oil as well as increasing intake of fruits, vegetables, whole grains and some red wine. Canola oil, which contains mostly monounsaturated fat, is a cheaper alternative to olive oil but may not be as effective since it does not have the polyphenols that the latter has. Research data show that adopting a Mediterranean diet can halve the risk of getting a heart attack in just two to four years.

Another advantage of replacing omega-6 fats, found in oils rich in polyunsaturated fatty acids, by olive oil is that the ratio between omega-6 and omega-3 fatty acids is reduced. The major fatty acid in olive oil is oleic acid, which is not an omega-6 but rather an omega-9 fatty acid. So, consuming olive oil instead of polyunsaturated fatty acids lowers the ratio of omega-6 and omega-3. One theory postulates that the rash of heart disease, cancer, diabetes and arthritis is due to a move away from the 1:1 ratio of those two acids which existed with our ancestors' diet.

Cancer prevention is another benefit of the Mediterranean diet. A study carried out at the University Hospital Germans Trias Pujol in Barcelona found that rats fed a diet containing 5% olive oil had a lower colon cancer rate than rats on a diet with 5% safflower oil. In fact, the lower rate was comparable to that of rats fed a diet containing 5% of omega-3 fatty acid-rich fish oil, which has previously been shown to reduce the risk of colon cancer. It is thought that antioxidants in olive oil afford some protection against cancer. In this respect, it's possible that brined olives, which have a higher concentration of phenolic antioxidants, such as apigenin, than olive oil may have more potent anti-cancer activities.

A report published in the Journal of Epidemiology and Community Health from the Institute of Health Sciences at Oxford University, indicates that olive oil was associated with a decreased risk of colon cancer whereas the opposite was true for a diet high in meat and low in vegetables. In fact, olive oil was found to be just as good as vegetables and fruits in preventing colon cancer.

Many studies have shown that by severely restricting the diet, the speed of ageing could be slowed down and lifespan extended in several organisms and mammals. This is believed to be due to increased activity of sirtuin enzymes. Adding olive oil to the diet could have a similar effect and is easier to do.

Scientists from Harvard Medical School and BIOMOL Research Laboratories in Philadelphia have found that certain polyphenols from fruits and vegetables, especially resveratrol found in red wine and quercetin in olive oil, extended the life of yeast cells by up to 70%. Researchers hope that these molecules might have the same effect on humans—protecting cells from damage and death and thus preventing disease and increasing longevity. It is already known that polyphenols have antioxidant properties and as such lower the risk of heart disease and cancer but their sirtuin enzyme stimulation may be even more important.

However, antioxidants may not be the answer to ageing, according to some scientists. In fact, a study published in a 2005 issue of the journal Science, found that damage to cells' DNA is the cause of ageing but this is not the result of oxidative stress and free radicals but rather that of programmed cell death.

The polyphenols in olive wastes, left after the oil has been pressed out, are being investigated as potential organic fungicides. Experiments carried out at the University of Bonn have shown that olive wastes inhibit the growth of molds such as *Botrytis cinerea* which damage grapes, strawberries and raspberries, *Fusarium culmorum*, a wheat blight and *Phytophtera infestans*, the fungus responsible for the potato famine in Ireland. These wastes could, therefore, become non-toxic, organic fungicides, which could be used even during harvesting.

However good olive oil is for you, remember it is still a fat and has twice the calorie content of carbohydrates or proteins. So, as always, moderation is the key.

PRUNES: MORE THAN A PURGATIVE!

Prunes are plums (Prunus domesticus) that have been allowed to dry either in the sun or by passing them through hot air at 85- 90 degrees Celsius for 18 hours. Plums that are most suitable for drying are those that have low water content; having less juice to evaporate reduces the risk of fermentation before the fruit has dried.

European plums are among the leading plum varieties which are often dried to make prunes. They are medium-sized, dark blue to red in colour, with a thick skin and yellow flesh. When dried, prunes weigh about one third that of the corresponding plums.

Plums appear to have originated near the Caspian Sea and the practice of drying them for preservation also started in the same area. California is now the largest producer of prunes in the world. To soften a prune, just allow it to soak in water for several hours.

Various sizes of prunes, now also known as dried plums, are available as well as pitted and non-pitted ones. Prune juice and prune puree are also available. Recently, the puree has been added to hamburgers and sausages not only to make them juicier but also to impart some antibacterial properties. When ground beef was mixed with 3% prune puree, it killed all the bacteria present within five days.

Prunes are a source of dietary fibre, antioxidants, carotenes, sorbitol, potassium, copper, boron, iron, potassium and magnesium, which together help digestion, cardiovascular health, glucose as well as bone metabolism, according to research at the University of Illinois.

As most people already know, prunes are a good source of fibre, both soluble and insoluble, with half a cup supplying a quarter of our daily requirement.

A study showed that men who ate twelve prunes per day had 20% more fecal mass, thanks to the laxative properties of the fruits. In fact, prunes are well known for their mild laxative effect, which has been attributed to their high fibre content. However, prune juice, which is filtered and so has little fibre, also has a laxative action. It could be that the laxative action is aided by phenolic compounds, sorbitol or caffeic acid found in prunes.

Soluble fibre, such as that which is found in prunes, has been shown to lower the level of the 'bad' LDL cholesterol without affecting the 'good' HDL cholesterol. A 2003 study, covering 10,000 people over 19 years, in the Archives of Internal Medicine showed that those eating more than twenty-one grams of fibre per day had 12% less coronary heart disease than those eating five grams or less daily. Those who ate the most water-soluble fibre had a 15% reduction of coronary heart disease risk.

A University of California at Davis study showed that adding 12 prunes to the daily diet increased the dietary fiber intake and lowered LDL cholesterol in those that had high levels to start with.

Both plums and prunes are rich in phenolic antioxidants such as chlorogenic acid and neochlorogenic acid, which have been shown to inhibit LDL oxidation, thus reducing plaque formation in the arteries.

Soluble fibre has also been found to help control blood glucose levels and aid in the treatment of type-2 diabetes.

The insoluble fibre in prunes helps speed up the passage of food in the intestine, thus reducing the risk of hemorrhoids and colon cancer.

In a test to measure the Oxygen Radical Absorbance Capacity (ORAC) at the Center On Ageing at Tufts University, prunes came out as the top antioxidant among several fruits and vegetables. Prunes are also rich in beta-carotenes which are fat-soluble antioxidants. Thirteen carotenoids, out of which seven are converted to vitamin A, have been found in prunes in a 2000 study at the University of Maryland.

Since antioxidants help destroy free radicals that can cause damage to DNA and cells of the body, prunes can help lower the risk of several diseases such as cancer and heart disease.

Prunes are also a good source of potassium, with half a cup containing 730mg of this mineral, which is necessary to help maintain normal blood pressure.

Vitamin K, which the body uses to control blood clotting, is rarely found in fruits or nuts, with the exception of prunes and some berries, according to a 2003 study in the Journal of the American Dietetics Association. People with frequent nosebleeds may be deficient in this vitamin, so eating plums and prunes may be helpful.

Since Vitamin K is involved in bone formation, it may also be responsible for decreasing osteoporosis and bone loss in postmenopausal women. A study in the Department of Nutritional Sciences at Oklahoma State University, and published in the Journal of American College of Nutrition in 2001, showed that a diet consisting of 25% prunes, given to rats with osteoporosis, reduced the disease and reversed the bone loss.

Dried prunes also contain boron, which is thought to be involved in preventing osteoporosis. A serving of prunes (100 g) fulfills the daily requirement for boron (2 to 3 mg).

In addition to being good sources of dietary fibre, plums and prunes were found to have high total concentrations of compounds that promote the development of healthy bacteria in the large intestine.

Pass the prunes, please!

RASPBERRIES: RED, BLACK OR YELLOW...
THEY'RE ALL GOOD FOR YOU!

When we buy raspberries in the supermarket they are usually red. However, there are other varieties, including a black one, which is indigenous to North America but, unlike its red cousin, is not sold commercially. Black raspberries are most often found growing wild. There are even yellow raspberries, but these are a recent addition to the family.

Raspberries are believed to have originated in East Asia and were mentioned in writings as early as 45 A.D.

The raspberry fruit consists of a collection of drupelets, each one being the little bump that one sees in a raspberry. It is, in fact, a minuscule fruit with flesh underneath a thin skin and a seed in the centre.

In addition to minerals and vitamins A, C and E as well as several of the B type such as B6, riboflavin, folate, niacin and pantothenic acid, raspberries contain anthocyanins, ellagitannins, salicylic acid, quercetin, catechins and fibre.

They are loaded with anthocyanins, with between 20 to 65 mg per 100 grams of fruit. The anthocyanins are responsible for the deep red or blue colour of berries and belong to the family of flavonoid antioxidants. The red colour of raspberries is due mainly to two anthocyanins, cyanidin-3-rutinoside and cyanidin-3-glucosylrutinoside, with darker berries containing more of the pigments.

Since they are strong antioxidants, anthocyanins help neutralise free radicals in the body that are involved in the initiation and development of diseases such as cancer and heart disease. These anthocyanins not only possess antioxidant properties but they also are antimicrobials with the ability to prevent the growth of bacteria and fungi, including the yeast Candida albicans which is responsible for vaginal infections.

In a 2000 paper in the Journal of the Science of Food and Agriculture, most of the antioxidant properties of raspberries are attributed to the anthocyanins and flavonoids, with only 10% coming from vitamin C.

Research from Finland shows that regular consumption of red raspberries can lower one's risk of heart disease. According to a paper published in the Journal of Agriculture and Food Chemistry in 2002, researchers at Glasgow University found that ellagitannins from raspberries are potent vasodilators. The same authors found that the amount of phytochemicals and antioxidants in fresh and frozen raspberries is very similar.

Ellagitannins have also been found to help reduce the risk of cancer, to control diabetes and, by mopping up free radicals in the brain, to reduce loss of memory and motor skills in old age.

Clinical tests have shown that ellagitannins, which are present mostly in the seeds of raspberries and strawberries, are converted by the body into the strong antioxidant, ellagic acid. According to the Agricultural Research Center of the USDA, free ellagic acid has also been found in other fruits, for example, in grapes, pomegranates and walnuts. Ellagic acid has been shown to have anticancer properties, especially against cancer of the esophagus and colon, by preventing cancer cell proliferation and tumour formation. Research carried out at Ohio State University and the M.D Anderson Cancer Centre of the University of Texas has shown that black raspberries limited both the initiation and progression of esophageal cancer.

A 2002 paper from the Department of Food Science at Cornell University in the Journal of Agriculture and Food Chemistry gives evidence of the dose-dependent inhibition of the proliferation of cancer cells by raspberry extracts. According to research carried out at the Medical University of South Carolina, ellagic acid kills prostate cancer cells in cultures and inhibits cancer in mice.

Just as with most fruits and vegetables, raspberries contain some salicylic acid, about 5 mg in three-quarters of a cup. It is quite possible that daily intake of salicylic acid from raspberries and other fruits could provide protection against heart disease, just as a daily dose of the closely related aspirin. The soluble fibre in the red berries also plays a role in lowering cholesterol.

Another important antioxidant in raspberries is quercetin, which human studies have shown can protect against lung diseases and allergies.

Raspberries also contain catechins; these are flavonol antioxidants which have been found to have anticancer properties.

The American Cancer Society recommends that one should consume a cup of fresh raspberries daily. However, they are expensive to buy and may not be available, especially in winter.

Raspberries have other uses too. Research carried out at Clemson University has led to the development of a topical skin cream made with raspberries to reduce skin cancer, scar formation and even ageing of the skin.

Is there any downside to consuming raspberries? Unfortunately, they do contain several pesticide and fungicide residues, with Captan, Iprodione and Vinclozolin being the most common ones.

There have also been several cases of cyclosporiasis in Ontario and elsewhere after consumption of fresh raspberries imported from Guatemala. The disease is characterized by nausea or vomiting followed by diarrhea. Although raspberries should always be thoroughly washed before eating, this does not totally eliminate the risk of contracting the disease.

Despite these minor drawbacks, raspberries are a good addition to the diet.

RHUBARB: NOT FOR EVERYONE!

Indigenous to Asia, rhubarb is a perennial plant belonging to the genus Rheum, comprising several species which are now grown in most areas of the world. Two species, R. rhabarbarum and R. rhaponticum, are commonly grown for cooking while two other species, R. officinale and R. palmatum, are mainly cultivated for their rhizomes and roots which when dried are used as medicine. Rhubarb is related to the garden sorrel, which is used in cooking because of its lemony taste.

The name 'rhubarb' is derived from the Latin words 'rha barbarum' since the Romans first found it growing on the banks of the Volga (Rha in Latin) which was, as far as they were concerned, barbarian territory! The name 'rheum' could also be derived from the Greek word 'rheo' which means 'to flow', in reference to its laxative properties!

The dried roots and rhizomes of the Chinese species (R. palmatum) have been used in traditional Chinese medicine to treat constipation and other stomach diseases as early as 2700 B.C.

Rhubarb was brought to Europe by Marco Polo on his return from China, towards the end of the 13th century. It was first grown in Italian gardens in the early 1600's as a medicinal plant but was only cultivated and used for making pies two centuries later.

Sometimes known as the 'pieplant', rhubarb is treated as a fruit although, botanically, it is a vegetable. Although very tart, several desserts can be made with it when sugar is added, such as crumbles or pies, on its own or in combination with strawberries, pears or ginger. It can also be used to make bread or jam, or simply mixed with custard or ice-cream. Rhubarb can even make a delicious rosé wine.

The only edible parts of the rhubarb plant are the thick, reddish stalks which research at Hamburg University Medical School has confirmed to be safe. The large leaves, on the other hand, contain oxalic acid which makes them poisonous. If consumed by animals or humans, the high levels of oxalic acid could cause the tongue and the throat to swell, thus hindering breathing. Realistically, however, an average man would have to eat about five kilograms of rhubarb leaves for them to become toxic, although you could become sick on consuming far less than that. The stalks can be eaten since they contain very little oxalate, especially if harvested in the spring. However, people who are apt to form kidney stones should not increase their intake of oxalates, which occur not only in rhubarb but also in spinach, blueberries and other produce. An increased consumption of oxalates will result in more being excreted in the urine, which may lead to kidney stone formation.

Rhubarb is rich in calcium with one cup containing about half the amount found in a cup of milk. However, the calcium is not easily absorbed by the body since a large part of it is combined with oxalic acid as the rather insoluble salt, calcium oxalate.

Although containing mostly water, rhubarb also has vitamins A and C, some potassium and is a good source of fibre. Due to the presence of fibre, rhubarb is effective at lowering cholesterol and triglycerides, according to research carried out with mice at the University of Alberta and Memorial University and published in the British Journal of Nutrition in 1999. However, this is not true if the mice are also diabetic!

Rhubarb root is a cathartic as a result of the presence of several anthraquinones such as emodine and rhein. Consuming a large amount of it could result in orange-coloured urine, since anthraquinones are generally orange in colour. Another purported medicinal property of rhubarb is its inhibition of inflammation of the pancreas.

Researchers from Guilin Municipal Medical College have found compounds in dried rhubarb roots, used in traditional Chinese medicine, that can fight the Severe Acute Respiratory Syndrome (SARS) coronavirus by preventing it from reproducing as a result of inactivation of an essential protease. It appears that they can also kill influenza and other respiratory viruses.

Rhubarb has found some unusual uses, partly because of the presence of oxalic acid, a moderately strong organic acid. It can be used to clean pans burnt during cooking and will make them shiny again. For the same reason, rhubarb should not be cooked in pots made of aluminum, copper or iron since the metals will turn the rhubarb brown on reacting with the oxalic acid.

Since rhubarb leaves are poisonous, boiling them with water and straining the liquid off will give a good insecticide, effective against aphids and other insects that feed on leaves. How about colouring your hair with rhubarb water? Well, it seems that in addition to being an insecticide, the liquid will also colour your hair from light to golden brown!

Now don't go shouting rhubarb after reading this!

ARTICHOKES: NOT FOR GOURMETS ONLY!

Originating in Southern Europe, the artichoke (Cynara scolymus) is a perennial plant belonging to the thistle family whose name is derived from 'articiocco', the Italian word for pinecone, because the latter resembles the globe at the top of the artichoke plant. The name 'cynara', on the other hand, belongs to a goddess who, according to mythology, was turned into an artichoke by a thunderbolt from Jupiter after he found himself tempted by her!

There are three types of artichokes but the one that is commonly found in the produce section of supermarkets is the globe artichoke, with its edible green head. The latter is actually the base of the undeveloped flower bud, which is produced only during the second and subsequent years of the plant's life. As for the other two, the Jerusalem and Chinese artichokes, they are tubers and only the roots are eaten.

To prepare globe artichokes for cooking, cut off the stem at the bottom of the globe and trim away the top quarter of the 'leaves' to remove the thorns that may hinder handling. Boil or steam the artichokes until they are tender.

The main challenge confronting artichoke neophytes is which part of the bulb to eat?

The edible parts are the somewhat bitter tasting flesh at the bottom of the 'leaves' and the fleshy middle part of the artichoke, to which the 'leaves' are attached, known as the heart. The so-called 'leaves' are really bracts or phyllaries. Starting from the base, each 'leaf' is removed and the soft fleshy bottom part is scraped off with the teeth while the rest of the 'leaf' is discarded. When all the 'leaves' have been eaten, the top layer of tiny leaves together with the delicious heart can then be eaten. The heart is also good pickled and the inner leafstalks can be used in soups and salads.

The artichoke was developed from the cardoon, another member of the thistle family, possibly by early Berber farmers. Artichokes have been cultivated for around 2,000 years and evidence for their use as food has been found in ancient archaeological ruins. Today, globe artichokes are cultivated mainly in Southern Europe and in California.

Nutritionally, artichokes are high in fibre, potassium, magnesium, vitamin C, folates, manganese, chromium, phosphorus and many phytochemicals.

The medicinal value of artichokes has been known for many centuries—even Pliny wrote about them. Artichokes have been used as an aphrodisiac, a diuretic, to detoxify the liver, improve bile formation, lower cholesterol and cleanse the blood. There are other uses as well, such as for the production of a yellow dye and as a substitute for rennet in cheese-making in some areas of Spain.

Modern research has confirmed many of the traditional medicinal uses of artichokes, especially its ability to regenerate liver cells, promote bile production and lower cholesterol.

Artichoke extracts have been shown to protect the liver from the nefarious effects of toxins from environmental pollutants and may also help regenerate damaged liver tissues. They have also been found to reduce fat build up in the livers of chronic drinkers. The protective effect is due to antioxidants in artichoke such as cynarin.

Artichokes have been used since ancient times as a remedy

for indigestion, which could be caused by inadequate bile flow. Double blind clinical studies by German researchers in 1994, and one in 2003 from the Department of Gastroenterology of the University of Essen, have shown that artichoke extract promotes bile flow and alleviates symptoms of dyspepsia.

In addition to helping relieve symptoms of dyspepsia, research carried out in the Department of Food Science and Technology at the University of Reading showed that artichoke leaf extract could also help patients suffering from irritable bowel syndrome.

A study published in a 1995 issue of the British Journal of Phytotherapy, on the treatment of patients with high blood cholesterol with artichoke juice, showed decreases in LDL cholesterol and total cholesterol but a significant increase in the 'good' HDL cholesterol. This has been attributed to cynarin and another related active component, 1,5-dicaffeoylquinic acid.

Other studies have found that artichoke extract lowered blood levels of cholesterol and triglycerides by an average of 12% each, thus confirming similar observations made as early as the 1930s.

Further confirmation came with a double blind clinical trial carried out in 1996, which showed that artichoke extract decreased cholesterol levels in patients having high initial levels. In fact, the higher the initial level of cholesterol, the bigger the drop, while the 'good' HDL cholesterol level tended to go up. It appears that artichoke extracts lowers cholesterol by reducing cholesterol synthesis in the liver as well as by increasing the decomposition of cholesterol to bile salts, which are then eliminated.

Artichoke extract is also being investigated for treatment in areas as diverse as cancer and HIV Aids.

One curious property of artichokes, according to a 1972 paper in the journal Science, is that, after eating an artichoke, water will taste sweet. This is due to cynarin, which has the ability to stimulate the taste buds in the tongue that are used to detect sweetness. Maybe this will lead to the development of compounds which, although not sweeteners themselves, will help make food taste sweet. How sweet it would be to be able to say goodbye to sugar!

BEETS: A SWEET VEGETABLE THAT'S HARD TO BEAT!

Beets (Beta vulgaris) originated from the Mediterranean area and are descended from a wild, leafy variety having only very thin roots. They were originally cultivated for their green leaves which were used not only as food but also medicinally to soothe aches. Delicious when cooked, beet leaves are high in beta-carotene and calcium. Beets with good-size rounded or elongated bulbs were only developed around the 16th century.

Although beets are mostly red in colour, some varieties are white, yellow or even multicoloured. The red, purple and blue colours of most vegetables, fruits and flowers are due to the presence of anthocyanins, which are potent antioxidants. These colours depend on the type of anthocyanin and on the acidity or alkalinity of the plant tissues. For example, beet juice changes from red to purple in an alkaline medium. In Byzantine times, according to an article in the International Journal of Dermatology, hair was treated with a mixture of lime (an alkali), Cretan earth, water, covered with beet leaves and then washed. A recipe for purple hair?

Beets are the sweetest of all vegetables. However, despite their high sugar content, they are relatively low in calories. Beets are a popular vegetable, used in salads, pickles and soups such as borscht but, for obvious reasons, are not recommended for diabetics.

Another member of the same family, sugar beets, were bred from beets in the 19th century and are grown strictly for sugar production. The impetus for using beets as a source of sugar came when Napoleon found his access to sugar cane from the French colonies blocked by the British navy.

Beets are a good source of folate, vitamins A and C, calcium, iron and fibre. Compared to other vegetables, the iron content is quite high. Folate occurs in higher levels in beets than in most other vegetables, with 150 mg in 100g of raw beets but only 2mg in pickled beets. One cup of boiled beets has about one-third of our daily requirement of folate. Canned beets, on the other hand, lose 30% of their folate content but retain all of their antioxidant activity, according to a 2004 study done at Cornell University and published in the Journal of Agricultural Food Chemistry.

The main pigment in beet juice is betanin which is an antioxidant. Regular consumption of red beets could, therefore, protect against diseases connected with oxidative stress, such as cancer, and also strengthen the immune system. For example, in South Africa, beets are given to people with HIV/Aids to boost their immune system.

Animals fed beet fibre were found to increase the activity of two antioxidant liver enzymes, glutathione peroxidase and glutathione-S-transferase. Free radicals that are generated in the liver, as a result of detoxification of harmful substances, are mopped up by these enzymes, thus reducing the risk of cancer. Furthermore, the animals had increased protection against heart disease since their total cholesterol and triglycerides dropped by 30% and 40% respectively while the 'good' HDL cholesterol went up appreciably.

It has also been shown that beet juice inhibits cell mutations caused by cancer-causing nitrosamines. These are formed from nitrites, which are obtained by the reduction of nitrates that are added to processed meats. Ironically, although beets themselves naturally contain nitrates, a beet salad eaten with your hot dog could protect you against colon cancer!

A 2002 study in the American Society for Clinical Nutrition showed that betaine, another compound found in beets, reduces plasma concentration of homocysteine, elevated levels of which are a potential risk factor in heart disease. Betaine, together with s-adenosylmethionine (SAM), folic acid, vitamins B6 and B12, is used to treat high levels of homocysteine.

Betaine can be used for treating mood disorders such as depression, which is due to low levels of serotonin. Treatment with betaine raises the level of SAM, which influences serotonin metabolism.

It has been observed that after consuming beets, 25% of people will produce red urine. At one time, this was feared to be a loss of blood but, later on, was shown to be a loss of pigments from beets, mainly betaine. Further studies on the urine of 100 subjects, using high-pressure liquid chromatography, showed that all samples contained the pigment except that, in many cases, the concentration was too low to show up.

According to BBC news, in July 2003 two beetroot farmers in Lincolnshire got a government grant to explore the possibility of marketing beets as an aphrodisiac. This intriguing property of beets is thought to be due to the presence of boron, which is involved in the making of sex hormones.

However, if you simply want to have a long and healthy life, according to the Talmud you should be "eating beetroot, drinking mead and bathing in the Euphrates"!

CELERY: BLOOD PRESSURE REGULATOR?

"Celery, raw develops the jaw,
But celery, stewed, is more quietly chewed"...Ogden Nash.

Celery (Apium graveolens), a member of the Umbelliferous family, which includes carrots and parsley, is native to the Mediterranean area and has been cultivated for over 3,000 years. Wild celery was mentioned in Homer's Odyssey and is still found today in areas stretching from Italy, through Asia Minor to Northern India. In ancient Greece, celery was awarded to winners at sporting events. It should not be confused with celeriac, which is the bulbous root of another variety of celery used in soups and stews. Nutritionally, celery is a very good source of vitamins A, C, K and B6, folate, potassium, calcium, manganese and fibre. It is somewhat high in sodium with about 50 mg in a medium stalk. Being 95% water, it is quite low in calories. In addition to the vitamins and minerals, celery also contains phthalides, coumarins and polyacetylenes, compounds that may help prevent heart disease and cancer.

Celery was first used as a medicine and then as food by the Greeks and Romans. Celery seeds, which are used medicinally as a diuretic and for treating rheumatoid arthritis, are collected from the dried fruits of the wild celery. A strongly flavoured oil is extracted from the seeds which contains phthalides such as 3-n-butylphthalide and sedanolide, coumarins, flavonoids, linoleic acid as well as volatile oils. In India, celery seed has been used for centuries as a treatment for poor digestion, water retention and arthritis. Research today is confirming some of the medicinal properties that have been traditionally associated with celery and its seeds.

Celery's ability to reduce blood pressure has been known for a long time. In Vietnam, for example, celery is a traditional remedy for high blood pressure. Researchers at the University of Chicago Medical Center have identified 3-n-butylphthalide as the compound responsible for lowering blood pressure. Incidentally, the same compound accounts for the peculiar taste and odour of celery. Animal studies showed that daily injection of 3-n-butylphthalide, equivalent to what is found in six stalks of celery, over a period of four weeks causes a 12-14% drop in systolic blood pressure as well as reducing cholesterol level by about 7%.

3-n-butylphthalide appears to lower blood pressure by acting as a mild diuretic, a vasodilator and by making blood vessels more elastic by reducing cholesterol and plaque formation. There was no alteration of sodium to potassium ratio in the blood, as there is with most prescribed diuretics. Thus, eating a few stalks of celery per day may help reduce your blood pressure, if it is high. On the negative side, it has been reported that people eating celery before or after strenuous exercise could develop allergic reactions!

3-n-butylphthalide in celery extracts has also shown promise in patients suffering from osteoarthritis and gout by reducing pain and increasing mobility. The only side effect observed was a diuretic action in some patients. It also appears to help gout patients by inhibiting xanthine oxidase, thus reducing the level of uric acid in the joints. The presence of Vitamin C may also help since it is a free-radical fighter and could reduce inflammation. It may, therefore, be beneficial for asthmatic and arthritic patients.

By their antioxidant action, coumarins in celery could also prevent cells from being damaged by free radicals and becoming cancerous while the presence of polyacetylenes could stop tumour cells from growing, if they have already been formed.

However, animal studies done on celery seed oil for the National Cancer Institute found that sedanolide was the most active of the anticancer compounds in celery and together with 3-n-butylphthalide, decreased tumour formation by 38-57%. Vegetables of the umbelliferous family, including celery, have some of the highest anticancer activities. It is also well known that compounds which increase the activity of glutathione S-transferase, such as phthalides in celery, are cancer inhibitors.

Both celery and its seeds contain compounds that may make the skin become sensitive to ultra violet light. For example, many cases of dermatitis occurred at two Oregon grocery stores when workers were exposed to sunlight after handling large quantities of celery during a celery sale. Research carried out at the Department of Dermatology of Lund University in Sweden, on a woman who developed phototoxic burn after visiting a suntan salon following consumption of celery root, has identified two psoralen derivatives as being the culprits.

Another peculiar observation is that some cats seem to get addicted to celery. One explanation is that the phthalides in celery have some sedative action similar to valium and cats like that!

Over the years, celery has acquired a reputation first as protection against hangovers, in Roman times, and more recently as an aphrodisiac. Both are probably myths, just like the belief of medieval magicians that putting some celery seeds in your shoes could make you fly!

EGGPLANTS: BERENGENAS OR MALA INSANA?

E ggplants come in many sizes, shapes and colours. They range from large, deep purple, oblong ones to small round, white ones resembling eggs. Although they are generally considered to be vegetables, botanically eggplants are really fruits.

The eggplant (Solanum melongena), also known as aubergine in French, a member of the Solanaceae or nightshade family, is thought to have originated about 4,000 years ago in North East India near the Burmese border. In fact, the name melongena is derived from a Sanskrit name for eggplant. According to the US Department of Agriculture, eggplants are still found growing wild in India although a secondary source appears to have been in China where smaller varieties were developed around the 5th century.

From India, the eggplant made its way to the Middle East and from there the Moors introduced it to Spain. In the 16th century, Spaniards thought that the eggplant was an aphrodisiac and so referred to it as 'Berengenas" or 'Apple of Love".

By the 18th century, it had become established as a vegetable in both France and Italy. However, since the eggplant is a member of the deadly nightshade family, Northern Europeans were suspicious of it and called it 'Mala insana' or 'mad apple', a corruption of the fruit's Italian name 'Melanzana'.

Eating it was thought to cause insanity! At one time, it was also called the 'apple of Sodom' since it was thought to cause fevers and epileptic fits in people who ate it. The botanist Linnaeus changed the original name of 'Solanum insanum' to 'Solanum melongena', meaning bad but soothing apple. Eggplants were introduced to the US by Thomas Jefferson from varieties sent from France.

Many popular dishes are made with eggplants, for example parmiggiana, ratatouille, eggplant caviar, moussaka, stuffed with lamb, baked with onions and tomatoes, curried and fried.

Eggplants are harvested when the fruit is still small, before seeds are formed which will make the fruits bitter. According to the Journal of Agricultural and Food Chemistry, this bitterness is due to phenolic compounds in the eggplant skin and seeds.

However, eggplants should not be peeled since most of the antioxidants are to be found in the peel. To get rid of the bitterness, the eggplant should be sliced, sprinkled with salt and allowed to drain for an hour or so. As a result of the process of osmosis, the salt draws out water as well as the bitter compounds. The slices can then be pressed dry with a paper towel which will remove even more moisture and bitterness.

Frying eggplant in oil results in the absorption of a lot of oil since the eggplant has a spongy texture. Baking or grilling is, therefore, preferable.

Although eggplants do not have particularly high levels of any vitamin, mineral or fat, they are quite filling and can be used as a meat substitute, supplying only a few calories.

Scientists at the US Department of Agriculture in Beltsville, Maryland have found that eggplants are rich in antioxidants such as caffeic and chlorogenic acids and flavonoids of the anthocyanin type such as nasunin. Nasunin (delphinidine-3-(p-coumaroylrutinoside)-5-glucoside)   was isolated by scientists at the Department of Molecular and Cell Biology at the University of California at Berkeley as purple crystals from the skin of eggplants.

Nasunin is a potent antioxidant and free radical scavenger, which protects cells from attack by free radicals. Plants form these antioxidants to protect themselves against oxidative stress from exposure to the elements and against infection by bacteria and fungi.

In a 2003 article in the Journal of Agricultural Food Chemistry, scientists from USDA in Beltsville found that chlorogenic acid (5-O-caffeoylquinic acid) was the predominant antioxidant compound in eggplants. It has anticancer, antimicrobial and antiviral properties.

The researchers also found that the Black magic cultivar grown commercially in North America has three times the amount of antioxidant phenolics compared to other cultivars.

The phenolic acids are also responsible for the bitter taste and the browning that occurs when eggplants are cut. The enzyme polyphenol oxidase triggers a phenolic reaction which produces brown pigments.

When rabbits bred to have high cholesterol were given eggplant juice, their blood cholesterol was reduced and the walls of their blood vessels became more relaxed, thus improving blood flow. This effect was due to nasunin and perhaps other phytonutrients as well.

Nasunin is also an iron chelator. Excess iron in the body is associated with increased free radical formation and an increased risk of cancer and heart disease. By chelating iron, nasunin reduces free radical formation thus resulting in less cellular damage and a decreased cancer risk. It also causes less free radical damage to joints resulting in a reduced risk of rheumatoid arthritis.

Being a potent oxygen radical scavenger, nasunin has been found to protect against lipid peroxidation of brain homogenates and could, therefore, help protect the brain during ageing.

Nasunin is one of many anthocyanins that are responsible for the intense colours of many fruits and vegetables, such as blueberries, blue grapes and red cabbage. Epidemiological investigations have indicated that the moderate consumption of anthocyanins such as those found in red wine or bilberry extracts, is associated with a lower risk of cardiovascular disease and improvement of visual function.

Is there any reason not to eat eggplant? It is possible that solanine, the alkaloid that is found in plants of the nightshade family such as tomatoes, peppers, potatoes and eggplants, may cause problems for people with osteoarthritis by preventing them from eliminating it from the gut. This may result in an accumulation of solanine which could exacerbate their osteoarthritis. Preliminary results suggest that exclusion of solanine from the diet could be of benefit. However, a strict double blind clinical testing has not been done. In any case, any effect of this treatment is only seen after six months on this exclusion diet. This approach can only been recommended to people suffering from severe osteoarthritis which has not responded to other treatments.

So, if you do not have osteoarthritis, why not try one of the many delicious dishes made with eggplant? You can be certain that it won't make you mad, as was once thought, but don't bet on it being an aphrodisiac either!

GREEN PEAS: NUTRITIONAL GREEN GIANTS!

P eas (Pisum sativum) are one of the earliest plants to have been domesticated, after wheat and barley. They appear to have originated in an area stretching from Eastern to Central Asia. The earliest evidence of humans collecting peas for food was found in a cave on the border between Thailand and Burma. By means of radiocarbon dating, these wild peas were found to be 9,750 years old. The cultivation of peas, on the other hand, started over 3,000 years ago and they are now produced commercially in England, the USA, China and India.

Tender varieties were developed in the 16th century so that they could be eaten fresh. While today, green peas are used as fresh vegetables, prior to the 16th century, they were used only after they had been dried. In Japan, a favourite snack to eat while drinking beer is fried green peas. This snack was also popular with Romans a couple of thousands of years ago!

Peas are members of the legume family. Unlike other plants, which need an external supply of nitrogen to grow, legumes have nodules on their roots which, with the help of a soil bacterium (Rhizobium spp.), can absorb and utilize the nitrogen from the air that has been absorbed by the soil. The bacteria fixes nitrogen into ammonium ions which the plant can use and, through a symbiotic relationship, the plant, in turn, supplies the bacteria with carbohydrates.

There are many varieties of peas including shelling peas, which can have smooth skins and are sold fresh and frozen, or wrinkled ones, which are mostly used for canning. Snow peas or 'mangetout' are eaten, together with their pods, when they are still flat with miniature peas inside. Sugar snap peas were developed twenty-five years ago by crossing snow peas with English green peas. They give crunchy pods with fully matured sweet peas inside and are eaten like green beans.

Another kitchen favourite is petit pois, which are green peas picked before they reach maturity, and so are smaller and sweeter. These delicate peas can be cooked simply by putting them on a few moist lettuce leaves in a covered pan, topped with another leaf and then heated at low heat until they become tender.

Although green peas are eaten when they are still immature, they can also be allowed to mature and dry on the vine. The resulting dried peas are known as marrowfat peas in England. When re-hydrated and mashed, they give the popular English mushy peas.

In North America, only about 5% of the green peas produced are sold fresh and the rest are either frozen or canned. Frozen peas taste and look better than the canned variety. However, the peas have to be frozen quickly after harvesting since their sugar will turn to starch.

Canned peas, first marketed by the Campbell Soup Co. in 1870, lose their bright green colour and turn olive-green since some of the chlorophyll is destroyed during the canning process. Artificial colouring, together with sugar and salt are added, to enhance the colour and taste.

Green peas are loaded with protein, folate and several other B vitamins, vitamin C, vitamin K, fibre and minerals such as iron, calcium, magnesium and zinc. Since peas belong to the legume family, they typically have a high protein, high fibre and low fat content. Among vegetables, they provide the highest amount of protein after lima beans. In fact, one cup of fresh peas provides more protein than one large egg.

Folate and vitamin B6 both lower blood homocysteine levels and so reduce the risk of cardiovascular disease and, together with fibre and potassium, help lower blood pressure and protect the heart. A diet low in potassium and high in sodium may be a contributory factor in high blood pressure. A cup of peas is a good source of potassium and may protect against hypertension. Peas also contain phytosterols which lower the 'bad' LDL cholesterol and further lower the risk of heart disease and stroke.

Vitamin K, which is found in peas and many green vegetables, is needed for good blood clotting ability and bone mineralization.

Green peas are also a good source of several B vitamins such as B1, B6, B2, B3, which are all involved in the metabolism of carbohydrate, protein and lipids. They are also one of the richest sources of insoluble fibre, which maintains a healthy alimentary tract and so protects against intestinal problems such as constipation and diverticulitis. Fresh green peas should also find favour with type-2 diabetics since the relatively low glycemic value and high fibre will control blood glucose and insulin levels after a meal.

Green peas contain iron and vitamin C which prevent iron deficiency and also provide a boost to the immune system. In addition, vitamin C and beta-carotene, which in the body is converted to vitamin A, are antioxidants that protect against free radical damage that could lead to heart disease and many types of cancer.

Peas have also another claim to fame unrelated to

cooking. The Austrian monk and botanist Gregor Mendel laid the foundation of modern genetics by discovering the basic principles of heredity from his plant-breeding experiments with peas.

MUSHROOMS: CANCER FIGHTERS!

Mushrooms have been used by hunter-gatherers since prehistoric times. Much later on, they acquired a special aura with the ancient Romans who referred to them as food for the gods and the early Egyptians who reserved them for their pharaohs.

It is estimated that there are over 150,000 species of mushrooms known today, many of which are edible and some toxic. Mushrooms should preferably be eaten cooked since the cell walls are fibrous and not easily digested. Furthermore, if toxins are present, cooking generally reduces their effect.

Although mushrooms are still collected in the wild, the most common mushroom in grocery stores, the white button mushrooms (Agaricus bisporus), are cultivated nowadays, following their introduction in France in the 17th century. More recently, brown strains of this species have been introduced on the market. These Crimini mushrooms are light brown in colour, and when allowed to mature, they give rise to the large Portabello mushrooms. Button mushrooms are usually harvested before the top or cap has opened. Specialty mushrooms such as Shiitake, Maitake and Reishi, long used in China and Japan as food and medicine, are now gaining popularity in North America, partly because of their medicinal properties.

Mushrooms are not vegetables but are rather the 'fruits' of certain fungi. They grow from a mass of branched filaments called a mycelium, using carbohydrates and proteins from decaying organic matter as food. Unlike green plants, they cannot use sunlight for energy and so may grow in the dark. They propagate themselves by releasing spores.

However, some mushrooms such as the Porcini cannot be cultivated since they are parasites living in the roots of trees from which they get their food.

Mushrooms are high in minerals such as selenium, copper, manganese, potassium, phosphorus and zinc.

Selenium is important for the immune, thyroid and male reproductive systems. Selenium works as a co-factor of glutathione peroxidase, a natural antioxidant produced by the body, and also with vitamin E in many other antioxidant systems in the body. These protect the body from damaging free radicals thus helping stave off cancer, especially prostate cancer, heart disease and arthritis. The National Cancer Institute is carrying out a 12-year study, the Selenium and Vitamin E Cancer Prevention Trial (SELECT), on 32,000 men to find out exactly how selenium and vitamin E protect against prostate cancer. Half a pound of button mushrooms, such as crimini, provides about one third of our daily requirement of selenium and may prove to be an important addition to a cancer-fighting diet.

Copper and manganese are trace minerals which act as co-factors for superoxide dismutase, another natural killer of free-radicals, found in the energy production centers of the cells, the mitochondria. Half a pound of mushrooms provide about one-third of our daily requirement of copper.

Mushrooms are also good sources of several important B vitamins such as riboflavin, pantothenic acid, niacin, thiamin, Vitamin B6 and folate, which are involved in carbohydrate, protein and lipid metabolism. Riboflavin may be effective in reducing the frequency of migraine headaches while pantothenic acid helps the adrenal glands and so can prevent fatigue during stressful times. Riboflavin also helps with good vision and in keeping the skin healthy. Pantothenic acid is involved in the formation of many hormones and also influences the nervous system.

Niacin helps reduce cholesterol while vitamin B6 lowers homocysteine levels, which could otherwise increase the risk of heart attacks and strokes. A 2004 issue of the Journal of Neurology, Neurosurgery and Psychiatry points out that consuming foods rich in niacin, such as mushrooms, could reduce the risk of Alzheimer's disease and the cognitive decline that generally occurs during ageing. Niacin is also involved in keeping the digestive and nervous systems functioning properly.

Years of research have shown that specialty mushrooms such as Reishi, Maitake and Shiitake, as well as the popular button mushrooms, possess anti-cancer properties, especially against breast cancer. Scientists believe this arises as a result of the inhibition of aromatase (also known as estrogen synthase), an enzyme necessary for the synthesis of estrogen. Thus by reducing the level of estrogen, mushrooms can reduce the risk of estrogen-driven cancers such as breast cancer. Some preliminary test-tube studies done at the Beckman Research Institute of the City of Hope in California, suggest that, of several mushrooms tested, fresh white button mushrooms were the most effective aromatase inhibitor and could, therefore, play a role in the treatment of or in reducing the risk of breast cancer in post-menopausal women. The other Agaricus mushrooms also had significant anti-aromatase properties. Animal and human studies are in the offing.

Just like other mushrooms, Shiitake mushrooms contain

glutamic acid, the sodium salt of which is monosodium glutamate, a flavour enhancer. Cooking them with other foods will increase the flavour while adding only a few calories.

Shiitake and Maitake mushrooms have been extensively studied in the East for their ability to boost the immune system and their reduction of cancer and heart disease risks.

Japanese scientists have isolated lentinan from shiitake mushrooms, which they claim can fight infection and slow progression of cancer by strengthening the immune system. Similar compounds inhibiting tumour growths have been isolated from Maitake mushrooms. A study at the New York Medical College indicated that they also killed test-tube samples of prostate cancer cells. Other studies carried out in Japan showed that rats fed Maitake mushrooms daily lowered their high blood pressure and cholesterol levels.

Some mushrooms grow by attaching themselves to trees and many of them produce natural antibiotics. The prime example of fungi as sources of antibiotics is, of course, penicillin, which is derived from the fungus, Penicillium notatum.

Why are fungi rich sources of antibiotics? Possibly because animals and fungi had a common ancestor over 460,000 years ago and so have developed similar defences against mutual enemies of microbial origin!

SWEET POTATOES: A STEP UP FROM POTATOES!

Unlike regular potatoes, which belong to the nightshade family, sweet potatoes (Ipomoea batatas) are members of the Convolvulaceae family. They also originate in Central and South America and have been cultivated by the Incas for thousands of years for food. Other uses included making red dyes for cloth and pottery by combining the juices of sweet potatoes and limes. The Incas' name for sweet potatoes was 'batatas', the origin of the word 'potato'.

Sweet potatoes were introduced to Europe by Christopher Columbus, after his trip to the Americas in 1492 and they then spread to Asia, Africa and North America. Although the English were suspicious of ordinary potatoes when they were first introduced, they readily took to sweet potatoes, which were regarded as a delicacy. In the US, sweet potatoes were a major source of food for the early settlers and for soldiers during the American Revolution.

There are over 400 varieties of sweet potatoes; the colour of their flesh varies from white to orange while the skin may be yellow, orange, red or purple. In cooking, sweet potatoes are very versatile and can be boiled, baked, fried as chips or candied.

Sweet potatoes rank as one of the top vegetables with regard to carotene content. In fact, they contain more beta-carotene than carrots! Besides beta-carotene, which is a precursor of vitamin A, sweet potatoes contain vitamins B6, C and E, minerals such as manganese, potassium, calcium, iron and copper, as well as plenty of dietary fibre. Unfortunately, most people in Canada tend to avoid sweet potatoes despite their wealth of nutrients.

Sweet potatoes contain antioxidant vitamins A, C and E as well as pigments that also have antioxidant properties. Pigments found in plants are generally antioxidants; their job is to protect the plants against damage caused by free radicals, formed by the action of the sun's UV rays on them. Free radicals also occur in the body but, in addition, can come from cigarette smoke and environmental pollutants. So, by eating sweet potatoes, as well as other vegetables and fruits, we get antioxidants which neutralize free radicals that damage the body's cells and increase the risk of getting heart disease, arthritis and cancer.

Sweet potatoes also contain vitamin B6, which lowers blood levels of homocysteine, thus further reducing the risk of heart disease and stroke.

Studies have shown that the presence of carotenes and dietary fibre in sweet potatoes helps type-2 diabetics stabilize their blood sugar and fight insulin resistance. Unlike ordinary potatoes, pasta or white bread, sweet potatoes have a low glycemic index and will not cause insulin peaks, which can lead to fatigue and increased fat storage by the body. Foods with a low glycemic index are absorbed slowly, thus giving rise to a moderate increase in the blood glucose level, followed by a gradual drop to normal values.

Animal studies at Kansas State University have shown that a carcinogen found in cigarette smoke, benzo(a)pyrene, causes a deficiency in vitamin A, which can lead to emphysema. However, when animals exposed to cigarette smoke were fed a diet rich in vitamin A, the incidence of emphysema dropped significantly. So, if you smoke or are exposed to cigarette smoke, you should protect yourself against getting emphysema by eating a diet rich in vitamin A. A cup of cooked sweet potatoes will supply about four times the recommended daily amount of vitamin A. Your best bet. though, is to stop smoking!

Although fruits and vegetables are generally high in potassium, sweet potatoes, together with bananas and ordinary potatoes, are the richest sources of potassium. Potassium, along with sodium, is involved in maintaining fluid and electrolyte balance. Since we generally have a higher intake of sodium, we should increase potassium in our diet, or reduce the amount of sodium, to maintain a balance between these two minerals. In addition, the presence of both calcium and potassium also helps in regulating heartbeat and blood pressure.

A comparison of the relative nutritional values of all vegetables, carried out by the Centre for Science in the Public Interest in 1992, showed that sweet potatoes are tops since they are high in fibre and complex carbohydrates, low in fat and have many nutrients. In fact, a small sweet potato will supply twice the required daily amount of vitamin A, 30% of vitamin C, fibre and several minerals, for only 140 calories. So, why not give it a try? There may also soon be available a nutritious pasta made with sweet potatoes and fortified with soya flour that has been developed at the University of Georgia.

If you want further incentives to try it, how about following the example of Japanese living in Okinawa who have the longest life expectancy as well as the highest percentage of centenarians in the world. What is their secret for longevity? Well, nothing really unusual except that they eat seven daily servings of grains and vegetables, in which sweet potatoes feature prominently, they are physically active and they do not smoke. There's a recipe we can all follow!

ZUCCHINI: ONE OF THE THREE SISTERS!

The wild squash from which zucchinis are derived originated in Central America, near Guatemala and Mexico, and archaeological evidence from an Oaxaca cave show that they were cultivated about 12,000 years ago. They belong to the Cucurbitaceae family as do melons and cucumbers. Maize, beans and squashes were the mainstay of pre-Columbian food in that part of the world and are known today as the three sisters.

Zucchinis and other squashes were brought to Europe by Christopher Columbus and other European explorers. Portuguese and Spanish explorers then introduced them to the rest of the world.

The zucchini was first grown in Italy for its edible blossoms but subsequently, Italians developed so many delicious dishes with the entire fruit that it became known as the Italian squash. The French, however, call it courgette and so do the English!

Zucchinis (Cucurbita pepo) are summer squashes and are harvested when they are still tender and immature. If allowed to grow further on the vine, they can become enormous but the flesh becomes inedible. The fruit varies in colour from dark green to light green and even yellow. Another variety of zucchini that has been developed in Italy is the cocozelle, which is shorter, light green and striped. Zucchini plants have both male and female flowers which, of course, have to be pollinated by insects.

The flesh of zucchinis is slightly sweet. However, occasionally a zucchini may turn out to be so bitter as to become inedible. This is due to natural toxins called cucurbitacins, which are quite common in wild varieties of squash but rare in cultivated ones. The very bitter taste is thought to arise as a result of an accidental crossing between cultivated and wild species. If you do come across a bitter zucchini, you should not eat it as it may cause vomiting or stomach cramps.

Zucchinis contain more than 95% water and so are quite low in calories when cooked without added oil, cheese or butter. Despite this, they are quite nutritious since they contain vitamin A, some B vitamins, vitamin C, minerals such as calcium, magnesium, copper, phosphorus and potassium, antioxidants such as beta-carotene and folic acid. It is not generally realized that one cup of zucchini has as much potassium as a banana!

When cooked with the peel, they will provide about four grams of fibre per cup, which is about 20% of our daily requirement.

Zucchinis may have some anticancer properties since some studies have shown that zucchini juice prevents the typical cell mutations that occur in cancer. Other studies carried out at the Department of Horticulture of Michigan State University have shown that some cucurbitacins inhibit the growth of colon, breast and lung cancer cell lines. Some of these compounds also show anti-inflammatory properties.

Zucchinis can help protect against cancer and heart disease in many ways. The fibre can help lower cholesterol levels and protect against colon cancer while magnesium and potassium can reduce high blood pressure. The presence of antioxidants such as vitamin C and beta-carotene can prevent oxidation of LDL cholesterol, which could otherwise lead to atherosclerosis. They could also protect against colon cancer as well as prevent inflammation that could lead to asthma and arthritis. The folic acid can help reduce homocysteine levels, thus reducing the risk of heart disease and stroke.

In addition to vitamin A, zucchinis also contain the carotenoid antioxidants, lutein and zeaxanthin. According to researchers at the Johns Hopkins University School of Medicine, a lack of lutein and zeaxanthin in the diet is associated with an increased risk of age-related macular degeneration. Zucchinis and green vegetables such as spinach should, therefore, be consumed in order to protect our sight, especially in old age.

According to an article published in the International Journal for Vitamin and Nutrition research in 2003, two phytosterols, sitosterol and stigmasterol, are found in high amounts in vegetables and fruits of the Cucurbitaceae family such as zucchinis, pumpkins, melons and cucumbers, where they occur mostly in the peel. These phytosterols, just like cholesterol, are transported by low-density lipoproteins (LDL) and are secreted unchanged in the bile. So, addition of plant sterols and stanols to the diet, especially when converted to their fat-soluble esters, has been shown to inhibit cholesterol absorption and lower serum cholesterol. Consuming plant sterol and stanol esters over the long term could reduce cholesterol, without any side effects, by up to 20%.

Plant sterols and stanols are structural components of plant membranes and occur in trace amounts in several plant species but in high amounts in some cereal species. Over 200 different plant sterols exist. The plant sterols and stanols have been studied extensively because of their ability to lower cholesterol. Two margarines enriched with esters of plant sterols and stanols are available on the market in the US and are effective at lowering cholesterol when one to three grams are consumed daily.

Did you know that zucchini and pumpkin plants have been shown by researchers at the Royal Military College at Kingston to be good at extracting DDT from contaminated soil? So, zucchinis may not only be good for nutrition but also for cleaning up the environment!

CORIANDER: MANNA FOR COOKS!

Coriander (Coriandrum sativum), a member of the Apiceae family which also includes parsley, is native to the Middle East where some of the oldest coriander seeds were discovered in a 8,000-year-old cave. Coriander must have spread to South East Asia quite early since their cultivation is mentioned in Sanskrit texts over 7,000 years ago. More recently, the seeds were discovered in 3,000-year-old Egyptian tombs.

Coriander is also mentioned in the Bible (Exodus, chapter 16, verse 31) in which manna was compared to it: "And the house of Israel called the name there of manna: and it was like coriander seeds, white; and the taste of it was like wafers made with honey".

The seeds and the fresh leaves have different flavours and both are used in cooking. The seeds have a sweetish, aromatic and lemony taste reminiscent of orange peel while the fresh leaves, known as cilantro, are very popular in Asian, Middle Eastern and Latin American cooking. Used in chutneys, salsa and guacamole, cilantro is said to be the most used of all flavouring herbs. Cilantro should not be cooked as heat will destroy its flavour but should rather be added as a garnish at the end of cooking. As the leaves lose their aroma when dried or frozen, it's best to keep them between sheets of paper towel in the fridge.

People have strong reactions towards fresh coriander,

most love it but some detest it! People who cannot stomach the leaves claim they taste soapy and have an unpleasant smell. This is believed to be a genetic trait or it could be the result of an allergy. In fact, an article in the journal Allergy, in 1979, reported the case of woman who developed an allergy to coriander after being exposed to it for 3 years. There is even a case of anaphylaxis to coriander that was discussed in a 1993 issue of the Journal of Allergy and Clinical Immunology.

As for the seeds, they are crushed and used in curry powder, pickling spices, sausages, cakes, breads and as a constituent of garam masala. Just like the fresh leaves, ground coriander is used extensively in Asian cooking. In Thailand, the root is also used in curries and meat dishes.

Since ground coriander loses its flavour within a few months, it's best to grind the seeds only when needed. Coriander was used as a spice in the kitchens of Medieval Europe mainly because its spicy and citrus flavour would mask the rotten taste of meat. Even today, coriander is used in the making of German sausages and other meat products. It is sometimes used in rye bread as a replacement for caraway. Since the Renaissance, one unusual use of coriander has been in the brewing of Belgium type beers.

In Scandinavia and Russia, it is also used as a flavour in liqueurs and in the making of gin. However, the largest use is in the making of curry powder and up to 40% of the world's production is used for that purpose.

Is coriander an aphrodisiac? There is no scientific data on this but there are at least three different sources that purport to show its use for that purpose. According to Pliny, a concoction made by adding crushed garlic and coriander leaves to wine, can act as an aphrodisiac. Similarly, during the 400 years of the Han dynasty in China, which started around 2007 B.C., coriander was used in love potions. In the Tales of the Arabian Nights, a childless merchant was cured by drinking a potion made of coriander. As far as is known, coriander is a stimulant for the appetite but not of the carnal kind!

In fact, coriander is a stimulant for digestion and also has antibacterial properties. It is used for relieving stomach upsets and other digestive problems.

In addition, coriander is added to strong-tasting medications to mask the taste and make them more palatable. It is also added to other medications that might irritate the stomach.

When ripe coriander seeds are distilled, about 1% of an essential oil, consisting of 60% of linalool and 20% of terpenes, is obtained. The oil has found some use in the perfume industry mainly because of its linalool content.

The taste of fresh cilantro is due to compounds that are long-chained aldehydes such as decanal and trans-2-tridecenal. The same compounds have been found in other herbs that have a similar taste to cilantro.

When cilantro leaves were distilled, the essential oil obtained was found to have antibacterial as well as antifungal properties. A paper in a 2004 issue of the Journal of Agricultural and Food Chemistry from the University of California at Berkeley showed that the volatile compounds in the fresh leaves of coriander have antibacterial activity against Salmonella choleraesuis bacteria. The bactericidal activity is due to their ability to act as surfactants.

Coriander has been used in several parts of the world in traditional medicine as a treatment for diabetes and high blood cholesterol, which some recent research is validating.

A 1999 article in the British Journal of Nutrition from the School of Biomedical Sciences at the University of Ulster demonstrated the presence of compounds in coriander that have antihyperglycemic properties and promoted insulin release in diabetic mice.

Coriander seeds have been shown to have cholesterol-lowering properties. A research paper, published in Plant Foods in Human Nutrition of 1997 from the University of Kerala, showed that coriander seeds reduced levels of total cholesterol and triglycerides in rats that were fed a high fat diet together with added cholesterol. The levels of the 'bad' cholesterol, low-density lipoprotein (LDL) and very low-density lipoprotein (VLDL), decreased significantly while the 'good' cholesterol, the high-density lipoprotein (HDL), increased.

According to a paper from the Technical University of Berlin, published in a 2002 issue of The European Food Research and Technology, high levels of sterols such as stigmasterol and beta-sitosterol, were found in extracts of coriander. Could this be the reason why coriander lowers blood cholesterol? Other studies have shown that sterols do lower blood cholesterol and, in fact, are added to some margarines for that purpose.

Today, oddly, coriander is also the name of a computer program used in the Linux Operating system!

MUSTARD: DO YOU CUT THE MUSTARD?

Mustard seeds have been used as a spice since antiquity and are even mentioned in 5,000 year-old Sanskrit writings. In the New Testament, there are three references to mustard seeds as being small and somewhat insignificant but nevertheless have the potential to grow into a big plant. The analogy referred to the growth of the kingdom of God.

The name 'mustard' comes from the latin 'mustum ardens' which translates into 'burning wine'. This refers to the way prepared mustard was made in France, by mixing the spicy hot paste obtained by crushing mustard seeds with must (the name given to unfermented grape juice). Mustard is a favourite condiment as it provides a lot of flavour with very few calories.

The mustard plant belongs to the Brassica family as do broccoli, cauliflower, cabbage and kale. Cooked mustard leaves are highly prized in some countries while the tiny seeds that the plants bear are popular the world over. The seeds can be white, brown or black and are obtained from three different varieties of mustard plants, the Brassica alba, Brassica juncea and Brassica nigra respectively. The mildest of the three varieties are the white mustard seeds which are, in fact, light yellow. The popular prepared yellow mustard is made from them, with some added turmeric to deepen the yellow colour. Black mustard is the most pungent and its oil is used for cooking in many parts of Asia. Brown mustard seeds, which originate from Northern India, but are now cultivated world wide, have a strong and acrid taste. They are used in the preparation of Dijon mustard.

Prepared mustards are made from crushed mustard seeds, wine, beer or vinegar, spices and salt. In some cases, the mixture is first simmered and then allowed to age before bottling.

Dijon mustard became popular in France because of its lower acidity resulting from the use of unripe grape juice called verjuice instead of vinegar in its preparation. Apart from Dijon mustard, there are other much sought after prepared mustards such as English, German, Meaux and sweet honey.

The pungency of mustard arises only when the seeds are crushed in the presence of water, as a result of a reaction between two compounds that they contain, myrosin and sinigrin. The strong taste and flavour dissipate rather quickly unless an acidic reagent such as vinegar is added. Nevertheless, prepared mustards will lose their flavour and spiciness on standing, even when the jars are unopened. Opened jars of mustard should be kept in the fridge to reduce the loss of flavour.

While prepared mustards from white seeds feel hot and spicy on the tongue, those made from the brown or black seeds are so hot that they can affect the nose and eyes as well. Cooking with mustard is not advisable since prolonged heating will reduce its pungent flavour; however, it can be added to a dish at the end of the cooking.

Before finding its place in the kitchen, mustard was used as a medicine as early as the 6th century B.C. by Pythagoras and later by Hippocrates. Mustard not only increases the appetite and digestion but also blood circulation. Today, many studies have shown that glucosinolates, in mustard seeds and in other brassicas as well, can be converted by the myrosinase enzyme into potent anti-cancer compounds called isothiocyanates. Animal studies have shown that these compounds are particularly effective against gastrointestinal cancers.

The seeds, oil and leaves of mustard contain many minerals such as phosphorus, iron, calcium, selenium and magnesium as well as monounsaturated fatty acids. Magnesium and especially selenium have been shown to have some anti-inflammatory properties. Selenium has been found to help reduce asthma attacks and may prevent some cancers while magnesium lowers blood pressure and protects against heart disease. However, our daily intake of these minerals and fats from prepared mustards is minimal. The exception is when people eat the cooked leaves or use the oil for cooking on a regular basis, as many do in Asia.

Although mustard oil has many health benefits for the heart, thanks to the high level of oleic acid, a monounsaturated fatty acid, it also contains a small amount of cis-13-docosenoic acid, commonly known as erucic acid. Consuming high levels of erucic acid could form fatty deposits in heart muscles, thus weakening them.

On the other hand, erucic acid mixed with oleic acid, gave Lorenzo's oil, made famous by the movie of the same name. That mixture saved the life of Lorenzo Odone who suffers from adrenoleukodystrophy (ALD). By the way, he is still alive in 2005 although unable to move. The treatment itself, which was ridiculed by experts, has now been shown to work when started early.

Scientists at the Genetics Department of Delhi University have succeeded in modifying the mustard plant using a combination of plant breeding and genetic engineering. First, using conventional plant breeding, they removed all the erucic acid. Then, they genetically modified the mustard plant to form a new strain yielding 75% oleic acid, 10% each of the essential unsaturated fatty acids, linoleic acid and omega-3 fatty acids. This new mustard oil is better for the heart than olive oil since it contains the same amount of oleic acid but also has omega-3 fatty acids which olive oil lacks. It may even be healthier than canola oil because of its higher oleic acid content. Vegetarians may thus have another source of heart-healthy omega-3 fatty acids, which are commonly found in nuts, seeds and fatty fish. Tests on the safety of the new oil are still in progress and some field trials will take place in the coming year.

Since mustard oil is commonly used in India, scientists are also trying, by genetic engineering, to increase its beta-carotene level. The latter gets converted to vitamin A in the body and can thus combat vitamin A deficiency, which is prevalent in children there. The technique for developing higher beta-carotene mustard seeds is the same as was used for developing yellow rice which also has higher level of beta carotene than white rice.

Scientists at the University of Guelph have found another use for yellow mustard. They have prepared a yellow mustard gum by mixing 90% of yellow mustard mucilage, a cheap soluble fibre from yellow mustard, with 10% of the expensive locust bean gum, which is used as a food stabilizer in the food industry. The product has much better gelling properties, is much cheaper and provides additional health benefits such as lower cholesterol and blood sugar levels.

You can avail yourself of another benefit of mustard next time you go cross-country skiing. Sprinkle some mustard powder inside your socks and, it is claimed, you will not get frostbite!

OREGANO: JOY OF THE MOUNTAIN!

People have used herbs in cooking and as medicine since the dawn of civilization. One of the most popular herbs, oregano (Origanum vulgare), chosen as the herb of the year for 2005, is thought to have originated in Greece. In fact, its name is derived from Greek and means 'joy of the mountain'. That's presumably because this perennial herb, a member of the mint family, grows wild and thrives in the mountainous regions of the Mediterranean area. To symbolize joy and happiness, newlyweds in Greece are often adorned with crowns of oregano.

Oregano leaves are commonly used in Greek, Italian and other cuisines from the Mediterranean area. The pungency of oregano lends itself well to this area's cooking, especially in tomato sauces, seafood and meat dishes, soups, stuffing, fried vegetables dishes with eggplant or zucchini and in pizzas.

Today, oregano is mostly associated with pizza, especially in North America. The history of pizza is illustrative of how a poor man's staple became a dish fit for kings! Although bread dough baked with some tomato paste on top has been a food for the poor for centuries in Italy, the first pizza was a richer version with added cheese, made for Queen Margherita when she and her husband, King Umberto, visited Naples in 1889.

Extraction of the leaves and flowers of oregano yields about 4% of an essential oil which contains two major compounds, carvacrol and thymol together with small amounts of borneol, limonene, linalool, triterpenoids, sterols and rosmarinic acid.

In addition to being a culinary herb, oregano has also been used as a herbal remedy. One of the constituents of oregano oil, thymol, has been used since ancient times to treat respiratory illnesses and coughs. Hippocrates, the father of modern medicine, prescribed oregano to cure stomach pain and to treat respiratory diseases.

In Europe, oregano, as well as marjoram, is still used to help clear sinuses, provide relief from laryngitis or coughing and preserve the voices of singers.

Oregano has potent antioxidant properties due partly to two compounds, thymol and rosmarinic acid. In laboratory tests, fresh oregano was shown to have more antioxidant capacity than blueberries, oranges or apples.

An article in Phytotherapy Research of 2002, from the School of Pharmacy of the University of London, showed that oregano from Italy and the Balkans, Origanum heracleoticum, is a strong antioxidant and inhibits bovine brain lipid peroxidation.

A study published in 2004 in the Archives of Animal Nutrition found that when rabbits were fed oregano oil, the antioxidant compounds delayed lipid oxidation in the tissues. However, this antioxidant effect was less than that obtained with Vitamin E.

It has been known since ancient times that oregano kills bacteria and it was, in fact, used in early Greece and Rome as a meat preservative.

The two components of the essential oil from oregano, carvacrol and thymol, are known to have antibacterial and antifungal properties. Studies carried out in Australia have indicated that oregano oil is effective against several bacteria including Escherichia coli and Staphylococcus aureus.

An experiment, carried out in the Department of Food

Science and Technology of the Agricultural University of Athens, and published in Applied Environmental Microbiology of 2000, involving inoculation of homemade eggplant salad with E. coli bacteria followed by addition of oregano oil, showed a drop in bacterial count which was dependent on the concentration of the oil, temperature and acidity.

Another article from the same school published in a 2001 issue of the Journal of Applied Microbiology showed that the addition of oregano oil to minced meat before packaging reduced spoilage by delaying microbial growth.

In tests done at the US Department of Agriculture in California on oil extracts from several spices and herbs, and published in the Journal of Food Protection in 2002, oregano oil was found to be among the most active against E. coli and Salmonella bacteria.

Oregano oil was also found to inhibit enteric parasites in adult patients, according to an article published in 2000 in Phytotherapy Research. In Mexico, oregano oil is used to treat people afflicted with the parasite Giardia.

Carvacrol has been shown, in vitro, to be more effective in inhibiting the growth of the fungus Candida albicans than calcium magnesium caprylate, a commonly used anti-fungal agent. At higher concentrations, oregano oil can kill toxic aflatoxin molds, which can grow in spoilt peanuts and peanut butter. So, it is possible that in future we may see oregano oil replace certain synthetic additives used in food processing to prevent spoilage.

There is some evidence from animal studies that oregano oil has anti-diabetic properties. A study published in the Journal of Ethnopharmacology in 2004 showed that an aqueous extract of oregano leaves normalized blood glucose levels in diabetic rats and that it did so without changing the basal plasma insulin concentrations.

However, everything is not rosy with oregano. Some people can develop an allergy to oregano, according to a 1996 Annals of Allergy and Asthma Immunology article from the University Hospital Clinic in Valencia, Spain. And what's pizza without a sprinkling of oregano on it?

PARSLEY: NOT JUST A GARNISH

Parsley (Petroselinum crispum), is a member of the Umbelliferae family which also includes carrots, celery, parsnip, dill, fennel and coriander. It is thought to have originated from the Mediterranean area and has been cultivated for over 2,000 years.

There are two main types of parsley: the curly leaf and the flat leaf variety, which is also known as Italian parsley. Chinese parsley, on the other hand, is in fact coriander, otherwise known as cilantro. Since flat leaf parsley has a more fragrant flavour and is less bitter than the curly leaf, it is preferred for cooking.

Parsley is commonly used in the cooking of many countries even though its origin is in the Middle East. Naturally, it features prominently in several dishes from this area such as tabouleh and falafel. In France, it is a major component of herb mixtures such as fines herbes and bouquet garni while in Italy, it forms part of the topping for osso buco. However, in North America, parsley is often used as a decorative garnish and generally not eaten.

Parsley contains many nutrients such as vitamins A and C, folate and iron as well as flavonoids and several beneficial volatile oils. A one-ounce serving of parsley has half of our recommended daily intake of vitamin C, one-third of vitamin A and one-tenth each of folate and iron.

Parsley contains many flavonoids such as apigenin, apiol

and luteolin. Research carried out at the Cancer Research Institute of the Slovak Academy of Sciences, showed that both apigenin and luteolin are strong antioxidants and protect DNA against attack by free radicals. When compared to several other flavonoids, luteolin was found to be the most potent in reducing damage done to DNA by oxidation. In addition, several studies point to luteolin as being active against many human cancer cell lines.

Similarly, researchers at the Institute of Food Safety and Toxicology of the Danish Veterinary and Food Administration in Copenhagen found that an intake of parsley over a two-week period increased the levels of two naturally occurring antioxidant enzymes, glutathione reductase and superoxide dismutase, which were shown to reduce damage to plasma proteins. Furthermore, the phytochemicals from parsley can prevent the formation of tumours by stimulating the protective phase II enzyme, glutathione transferase. This is a detoxifying enzyme that speeds up the reaction of glutathione with reactive cancer-causing species to form less toxic compounds that dissolve in water and can thus be excreted easily.

When applied topically to mice, apigenin has been found to block development of skin cancer by U.V light. Of 21 synthetic and natural flavonoids tested in the laboratory against human breast cancer cells, apigenin was found to be the most potent.

High levels of apigenin have been shown in an in vitro Dutch study, published in the American Journal of Clinical Nutrition, to inhibit platelet aggregation, which could lead to cardiovascular diseases. However, when volunteers were fed five grams of parsley daily, over a two-week period, no appreciable effect on platelet aggregation was observed! This could indicate that dietary intake of parsley cannot produce the high plasma levels of apigenin required to show a reduction in platelet aggregation.

One of the most important of the volatile oils in parsley is the alkaloid myristicin, which has been found to possess some hallucinogenic properties.

Myristicin also occurs in nutmeg; the latter has been used in large amounts as a recreational stimulant in some U.S prisons! The psychoactive and hallucinogenic activities of myristicin are thought to be due to its conversion to amphetamines in the body.

Animal studies have shown that myristicin neutralizes benzopyrenes, cancer-causing compounds which are found in smoke and which tend to accumulate in grilled meats such as hamburgers and steaks. So why not add a sprig of parsley next time you grill your hamburger?

Synthetic antioxidants such as butylated hydroxytoluene (BHT) and butylated hydroxyanisole (BHA) have been added to food to prevent lipid oxidation, which can result in undesirable flavours and decomposition products. However, consumers are rather wary of them, so scientists are now investigating the use of natural antioxidants, such as those from parsley, rosemary and sage, as possible replacements. Incidentally, luteolin is a more potent antioxidant than BHT and it may be even stronger than vitamin E.

The apiol in parsley is responsible for its diuretic activity and so can be used to increase urination in cases where there is water accumulation in the body. In fact, German physicians prescribe parsley seed tea to reduce fluid build-up in people with high blood pressure.

Allergy sufferers may also be helped by parsley. Research published in the Journal of Allergy and Clinical Immunology shows that parsley can prevent the secretion of histamine, the compound that is responsible for triggering allergic reactions in the body.

Parsley is also rich in chlorophyll and natural oils, which make it an effective breath freshener. So, if you have been feasting on garlic, chew on some parsley to sweeten your breath!

ACRYLAMIDE: A TEMPEST IN A...COFFEE POT?

Researchers from Stockholm University dropped a bombshell in April 2002 when they announced the discovery of a potential cancer-causing agent, called acrylamide, in several popular foods such as potato chips, French fries and bread. Subsequently, it was also found, but at lower levels, in coffee, baked goods, breakfast cereals, toast, pastries, pretzels, popcorn, peanut butter, biscuits and commercial fried chicken. More recently, it has even been found in prune juice and black olives. However, no acrylamide has to date been detected in raw vegetables, fruits or boiled foods.

What got people worried is that acrylamide is judged to be a potential human carcinogen. Animal studies done by the International Agency for Research on Cancer show that it causes gene mutations and stomach tumours. In addition, scientists at the City of Hope National Medical Centre have found that acrylamide can cause the mutation of DNA, a first step in cancer formation.

It has also caused damage to the nervous system in workers who had been overexposed to the compound in the workplace. Acrylamide is used industrially in the manufacture of chemicals, dyes and polyacrylamide plastics, which are sometimes used for the purification of drinking water.

So, how is acrylamide formed in food? According to a paper published in 2002 by D. Mottram in the journal Nature, acrylamide is the result of a reaction between asparagine, an amino acid found in potatoes and cereals, and a reducing sugar, such as dextrose, at temperatures above 125 degrees Celsius. This is known to organic chemists as the Maillard reaction and normally it adds colour, aroma and flavour to cooked foods.

Since high levels of asparagine are found mainly in plants, where it is needed for growth, fried or baked foods made with plant material rich in carbohydrates, such as potatoes and flour, will contain larger amounts of acrylamide than fish, meat or dairy products. The level in potato chips can be a hundred times higher than in bread or in drinking water where the allowable limit established by the World Health Organization is 0.5 part per billion.

It has been found that most of the acrylamide in food is formed towards the end of the baking, frying or roasting process when the temperature is at its highest and the water content at its lowest. The higher the temperature at which food is processed, the higher the level of acrylamide. For example, when cooked at 175 degrees Celsius, French fries contain about 300 micrograms of acrylamide per kilogram of potatoes while at 180 degrees Celsius, the level can go up to 1,100 micrograms per kilogram. The one known exception to this is with the roasting of coffee beans where the acrylamide level actually falls near the end of roasting.

In view of the potential dangers that daily ingestion of substantial amounts of acrylamide could represent, scientists are exploring ways to reduce the levels in foods. For example, adding the enzyme L-asparaginase to dough to degrade asparagine before baking, lowers the level in bread and pastries. Reduced levels are also seen in baked or fried potatoes when varieties of potatoes containing less reducing sugars are used. Incidentally, these sugars tend to increase when potatoes are stored below 8 degrees Celsius for long periods. Soaking sliced potatoes in water at room temperature for an hour or so prior to cooking has also yielded good results.

In an article published in 2004 in the Journal of Agriculture and Food Chemistry, scientists at the Swiss Federal Institute of Technology found that substituting ammonium hydrogen carbonate for sodium bicarbonate in baking reduced the level of acrylamide. A similar reduction was observed when citric acid was added to dough or when reducing sugars were replaced by sucrose.

How serious is the threat posed by acrylamide to our health? Studies done on seven thousand food items showed that the average intake of acrylamide in a typical Western diet amounts to 26 micrograms per day, with coffee contributing about half of that. This is at least 1,000 times less than the doses that are known to cause mammary gland tumours and reproductive problems in laboratory animals.

In a 2005 issue of the Journal of the American Medical Association, researchers from Harvard School of Public Health and the Karolinska Institute in Stockholm confirmed that acrylamide in our diet does not increase the risk of breast cancer. Earlier studies by L. Mucci at Harvard University have shown no link between dietary acrylamide and the risk of getting bladder, kidney or bowel cancer.

So, is all this just a tempest in a...coffee pot? Perhaps, although a few of these studies are somewhat contradictory! For example the U.S Centre for Evaluation of Risks to Human Reproduction has indicated that reproduction problems are unlikely as a result of consuming acrylamide in a regular diet. However, research carried out in 2003 at the Institute for Biomedical and Pharmaceutical research in Nuremberg has shown that 10 to 50% of a pregnant woman's blood level of acrylamide could be passed on to the fetus through the placenta. They went as far as to advise pregnant women to cut back on French fries and chips. Perhaps coffee should be added to this list too.

MEAT: TO BARBEQUE OR NOT TO BARBEQUE?

For most of us, there is nothing more enjoyable in the summer months than having a barbeque! However, let's say it right at the beginning: barbequing food, especially meat, is not a healthy way of cooking, if done on a regular basis! According to the American Institute for Cancer, the risk of stomach and colon cancer may be increased by an abundance of barbequed meat in the diet. However, there is a lot we can do to make barbequed food safer for us to enjoy.

We should always choose lean cuts of meat and any excess fat should be trimmed off before marinating. As for chicken, the skin should be removed first. Small portions of meat or fish should be used and supplemented with vegetables that are also delicious when grilled, such as mushrooms, onions, peppers, tomatoes and zucchini. You can even barbeque some fruits—mangoes, pineapples and peaches come to mind—to add to the meal or for dessert.

Meat or fish should be cooked thoroughly, so as to kill all bacteria, but it should not be charred! Barbequing fatty meat or fish can form cancer-causing compounds called polycyclic aromatic hydrocarbons. They are formed when the meat is charred or when fat drips on the charcoal and the resulting smoke deposits cancer-causing compounds on the meat.

Furthermore, on heating meat to high temperatures, amino acids, which are part of all proteins, react with creatine found in muscles to form other carcinogens called heterocyclic aromatic amines. More of these compounds are formed the longer the meat is fried or barbequed and the higher the temperature. In fact, a study found that well-done meat produces ten times more heterocyclic amines than meat which is less well cooked. However, cooking for a short period at low heat will not produce these harmful compounds, nor are they formed when vegetables or fruits are grilled.

Cooking should, therefore, be done without burning the food so as to reduce the risk of cancer. Even grilling potatoes and other foods high in carbohydrates can produce acrylamide, another carcinogenic compound.

Epidemiological studies have shown that people who eat their meat well done have three times the stomach cancer risk of those who enjoy it rare. A few other studies have shown that a high consumption of well-done meat, either barbequed or fried, increases the risk of breast, colorectal, lung and pancreatic cancers.

Research published in The American Journal of Epidemiology in 2003 showed that consumption of well-done red meat was positively associated with colon cancer and was due to heterocyclic amines in the meat.

Other research carried out at the National Cancer Institute, The University of Nebraska and Louisiana State University, and published in the International Journal of Cancer in 1998, indicates that barbequing or grilling meat led to an increased risk of stomach and esophageal cancers, in addition to colon cancer.

The future is not all grim, however, for those who like to barbeque. A study carried out at Lawrence Livermore National Laboratory, and published in a 2000 issue of the Journal of the National Cancer Institute, showed that formation of heterocyclic aromatic amines is reduced when making hamburgers by cooking them at a lower temperature and by flipping them often.

According to research published in the Journal of Food and Agricultural Chemistry, adding cherries or blueberries to meat before making hamburgers reduces the heterocyclic amines content of the burgers when cooked. This is due to the fruits' antioxidant properties, which inhibit formation of the amines. It was thus found that cherry hamburgers containing 11% cherries had 70% less of these carcinogenic amines. However, adding barbeque sauce to meat increases the heterocyclic amines content of grilled meat by up to 300%!

One study had earlier found that women who like their meat very well done had twice the risk of breast cancer compared to those who like it rare or medium. However, research published in 1999 in the International Journal of Cancer suggests that heterocyclic amines may not be a major cause of breast cancer!

Can meat itself, irrespective of the way it is prepared, be a cancer risk? According to a study carried out by the Fred Hutchinson Cancer Research Centre, the University of Utah Medical School and the Kaiser Permanente Medical Research Program, the total amount of both red and white meat consumed did not increase the colon cancer risk. Besides, totally eliminating red meat from the diet may lead to a deficiency of vitamin B12, iron and zinc.

On the other hand, research carried out in England and published in the British Medical Journal showed that, compared to meat eaters, vegetarians were 20% less likely to die before the age of 65 and 40% less likely to die from cancer. However, there is a drawback: according to researchers at the University of Massachusetts, whose paper appeared in The Journal of Clinical Endocrinology and Metabolism, a low protein diet is conducive to a low testosterone level, which is linked to a reduction in sexual functions!

EGGS: GET CRACKING!

Eggs have long been a staple of man's diet. They are highly nutritious since they are a complete protein food, which means that they contain all the nine essential amino acids that the body cannot make. Eggs are also low in saturated fats and contain most of the minerals and vitamins that we need, except for vitamin C. Despite this, eggs are still regarded with suspicion because of their high cholesterol level; an average yolk does contain about 213 mg. The egg white, on the other hand, contains no cholesterol.

Studies in the seventies showed a link between high blood cholesterol level and an increasing risk of cardiovascular disease. Since eggs are high in cholesterol, the advice has been to limit egg consumption, especially the yolk.

However, later research showed that dietary cholesterol has only a small effect on blood cholesterol. In a paper published in the Journal of the American Medical Association in 1999, scientists from Harvard School of Public Health found no correlation between consumption of eggs and cardiovascular disease, after following nurses and health professionals for 8-14 years. There was no increase in relative risk even among those who consumed more than two eggs a day, compared to those who did not eat any. However, they did find that there was an increased risk of coronary heart disease in diabetics who had a higher than average egg consumption. Their conclusion was that an egg a day is not likely to have any significant impact on the risk of coronary heart disease in healthy individuals.

Further confirmation came when an epidemiological study, carried out at the University of Michigan at East Lansing and published in the Journal of the American College of Nutrition in 2000, concluded that there was no relation between dietary cholesterol and blood cholesterol levels, after making adjustments for lifestyle and demographic variables. It found that those consuming four eggs per week had slightly *lower* blood cholesterol levels compared to those eating one egg per week!

So, it would appear that the benefits derived from the nutrients in eggs outweigh the adverse effects from their high cholesterol content.

However, some scientists were not completely convinced. Since egg consumption has been found, from several studies, to have little effect on increasing the risk of heart disease, is it possible, they argued, that eggs could increase the 'bad' LDL cholesterol but at the same time also increase the 'good' HDL cholesterol? In other words, could the adverse effects of egg consumption on total and LDL-cholesterol be somewhat mitigated by the beneficial effects on HDL-cholesterol? This is indeed what M.B. Katan at Wageningen University in the Netherlands found in 2001, on carrying out an epidemiological study on data that were available in the literature. He found that dietary cholesterol did raise the ratio of total to HDL cholesterol, thus adversely impacting the cholesterol profile.

The ratio of total cholesterol to HDL-cholesterol involves the interplay between the negative impact of LDL cholesterol and the positive one of HDL cholesterol on the risk of heart disease; consequently, he argues that this ratio is a better predictor of heart disease risk than the corresponding individual values.

It is perhaps not surprising that the American Heart

Association is still walking a cautious line, recommending a maximum of 300 mg per day of cholesterol from food, which could include an egg a day for healthy people.

The risk associated with egg consumption has to be balanced with its value as a cheap source of important nutrients including the omega-3 fatty acid, docosahexaenoic acid (DHA). DHA is needed for proper brain development in babies and for maintaining normal brain function in adults. A lack of DHA in infants hinders learning ability and in older people may lead to cognitive decline. Deficiency in DHA has also been linked to depression and an increasing risk of myocardial infarction. DHA is found in fatty fish such as tuna and mackerel, meat and in mother's milk but not in many infant formulas.

By feeding hens special diets containing flaxseed, kelp or canola, eggs containing more omega-3 fatty acids, iodine and vitamin E respectively, are now available, but the additional health benefits of these 'designer' eggs are still undetermined. Experiments carried out at the University of Guelph by B.G. Holub, and published in the Journal of the American College of Nutrition, showed that adding 10% of ground flaxseed to hens' diets can increase the DHA content of their eggs by 60% without changing the concentration of cholesterol. The eggs also had a very high increase in their alpha-linolenic acid content. Feeding four of these eggs to male volunteers daily for two weeks resulted in no change in their total cholesterol, high-density lipoprotein or triglyceride blood concentrations. It did, however, increase their total omega-3 fatty acids and DHA levels, thus providing another important source of these acids.

If a marigold extract is added instead to their diet, the hens will lay eggs that have a high level of lutein, which is needed for healthy eyes.

Egg yolks are the richest dietary source of choline, a B vitamin that could increase memory and has been labeled a 'brain food'. Other good sources of choline are beefsteak, cauliflower, iceberg lettuce, beans, peanuts and potatoes. There is some evidence that supplementing the diet of pregnant rats with additional choline can affect brain development in the offspring so as to make learning easier later on in life. Scientists at Duke University and at the University of North Carolina at Chapel Hill suspect that prenatal choline may even protect against changes in the brain that could lead to senility in old age. Their advice to pregnant women is to have a balanced diet with one or two eggs daily to ensure an adequate choline intake.

It has been known for sometime now that choline plays a role in liver function and cardiovascular health; it prevents fat from accumulating in the liver and is involved in the metabolism of fat and cholesterol. Even though choline is part of every cell and is synthesized by the liver from the amino acid methionine, we may not be getting the half a gram per day that is recommended by the Institute of Medicine in Washington, D.C., especially if we cut eggs from our diet.

So, eggs are a healthy addition to the diet as long as they are consumed in moderation. In fact, you may even lose weight since research has shown that women who consume eggs daily tend to eat fewer calories overall!

HIGH BLOOD PRESSURE: DIET AND EXERCISE WORK

Currently, it is estimated that, world wide, over 7 million deaths are due to high blood pressure. But by 2025, a staggering total of 1.5 billion people, one in three adults over 20, will suffer from it. So, what is this scourge?

Blood pressure (BP) is the force exerted by blood on the walls of the arteries as it is pumped by the heart and is usually measured in millimeters of mercury. Although a normal BP would be around 120/80, it tends to rise with age because of the reduced elasticity of the arteries. People having a BP greater than 120/80 and lower than 140/90 are considered to be prehypertensive. On the other hand, a patient suffering from hypertension will have a consistently high BP, usually above 140/90.

The top number is the systolic BP and is the maximum pressure in the arteries when the heart beats and pushes blood out into the body. The bottom number is the diastolic BP and is the force of the blood when the heart is at rest in between beats.

A high BP increases the risk of heart disease, stroke, aneurysm, eye damage and can lead to kidney disease.

To reduce these risks, especially that of developing cardiovascular diseases, it is necessary to lower BP. That can be done quite effectively by lifestyle and dietary changes. If you are overweight, even a relatively small loss in weight can result in a significant reduction in systolic and diastolic BP. It has been observed that the greatest reduction in BP occurs after losing the first twelve pounds.

A 2004 study in the Archives of Internal Medicine showed that sedentary and overweight patients with mild hypertension could control their BP by exercising and losing weight. The exercise involved jogging, cycling or brisk walking for half an hour three to four times per week and, on its own, reduced BP significantly. Other studies have shown that aerobic exercise reduces BP in hypertensive people as well as in those with normal BP, but it seems any exercise will do as long as it is done on a regular basis. However, when exercise was combined with a dieting program leading to a significant weight loss, it triggered an even bigger decrease in BP.

There is a lot of scientific evidence showing that a link exists between salt (sodium chloride) consumption and BP. Countries with traditionally high salt consumption, such as Japan, have higher BP than those with low salt intake, such as those in Africa.

The effect of sodium intake on BP was studied in the Dietary Approaches to Stop Hypertension (DASH)-sodium trial published in a 2001 issue of the Annals of Internal Medicine. This randomized feeding study of patients with untreated hypertension showed that a careful diet reduced BP; however, a greater reduction in BP occurred when sodium in the diet was reduced too. Even people who were not hypertensive achieved a reduction in their BP by consuming less sodium. Since most people already consume too much salt, reducing our salt intake to a maximum of one teaspoon per day is a precautionary move that we should all make. So, if you have high BP, try not to add salt to your food and avoid canned vegetables, frozen prepared foods, pizzas and fast foods, processed meats and snacks, which all have high levels of salt.

Reducing sodium alone is sometimes not enough to lower BP but must be accompanied by an increase in potassium. In fact, an early paper from the Department of Medicine at Johns Hopkins University concluded that low potassium consumption in the diet may result in high BP and that these cases should be treated with increased potassium, especially for those having difficulty reducing their sodium intake. Foods rich in potassium include bananas, pumpkins, oranges, peas, beans, potatoes, sweet potatoes, prunes, avocadoes and tomatoes.

A paper from the Erasmus University Medical School in the Netherlands, published in the British Medical Journal in 1994, showed that replacing sodium by a combination of low sodium, high potassium and high magnesium salts lowered BP in older patients. Foods rich in magnesium are beans, soy milk, leafy greens, spinach, broccoli, scallops, whole wheat, nuts and seeds.

More recently, studies have indicated that hypertensive patients consumed less calcium in their diet. In addition, an article in The American Journal of Clinical Nutrition in 2000, from the University Hospital of Tromso, Norway, showed that increasing calcium intake reduces BP. Good sources of calcium are milk and milk products (low fat), salmon, sardines, spinach, broccoli and tofu.

According to research on the DASH diet, people with high BP can lower it by a diet rich in fruits, vegetables, low-fat dairy products, whole grains, fish, chicken and nuts, while keeping to a minimum the consumption of saturated fat, red meat, sugar and salt.

An early study in the American Journal of Clinical Nutrition in 1988 from Harvard Medical School showed that strict vegetarians and lactovegetarians have lower BP than the general population, even after making allowances for weight, sex and age. It found that their low BP could not be explained by the lower consumption of animal products, carbohydrates or different types of fat but rather by the higher intake of nutrients from fruits and vegetables.

There are many vegetables that have traditionally been used to lower BP. For example, celery has long been used in Vietnam to treat hypertensive patients; eating just a few stalks of celery daily can lower your BP. An animal study carried out at the University of Chicago Medical Centre showed that a compound found in celery, 3-n-butylphthalide, is responsible for the reduction in blood pressure.

Eating garlic, as little as one clove per day, and onion has also been shown to be beneficial for lowering BP.

Tomatoes contain gamma amino butyric acid, another compound that can lower BP. Other vegetables, such as carrots and broccoli, and spices such as saffron, black pepper, basil, oregano, fennel, and tarragon can also help to lower BP.

Although we don't have to become vegetarians to lower our BP, we can adapt the DASH diet by making whole grains, brown rice, beans, vegetables and fruits the central part of our diet with only an occasional use of meat. This will reduce our intake of saturated fats, which, by increasing LDL cholesterol, can form plaques in arteries, thus narrowing them and increasing BP.

A 2002 article in the journal Circulation from the Department of Physiological Science of the University of California at Los Angeles, showed that three weeks on a low-fat and high-fibre diet, combined with daily exercise of about one hour in duration, decreased BP significantly.

Several studies show the beneficial effect of fish oils on BP. For example, a 1993 study in the Archives of Internal Medicine by the Department of Medicine of Johns Hopkins University showed that a relatively high dose of omega-3 fatty acids from fish oil could lower BP in patients whose hypertension had not been treated. However, according to an article in Hypertension from The University of Western Australia, it appears that of the two major omega-3 fatty acids that are found in fish oil, only docosahexaenoic acid (DHA), but not eicosapentaenoic acid (EPA), lowers BP in people.

A 1999 Spanish study in the same journal linked hypertension to the breakdown of oils used for frying. Consuming the many compounds formed when foods are fried in oil at a high temperature could increase BP. However, the study found that BP was inversely related to the blood concentration of monounsaturated fatty acids, commonly found in olive and canola oils.

Many other components of the diet can reduce BP. For example, a study on the role of isoflavones from soy on BP, published in the American Journal of Clinical Nutrition in 2002 from researchers at the Universities of Toronto and Guelph, showed a soy diet reduced BP moderately. Further evidence came from another paper in the American Society for Nutritional Sciences Journal of Nutrition in 2002, from a group at the Schools of Medicine of Zaragoza and Creteil, showing that soy milk, consumed at the rate of 1L per day, reduced BP in hypertensive patients.

An experiment at the University of Minnesota Medical School, published in the Journal of Family Practice of 2002, comparing oat with wheat cereals, found that the soluble fibre in oats could reduce BP and the risk of cardiovascular disease.

It seems that even the lowly potato can reduce BP. In a paper published in the 2005 issue of the Journal of Agricultural and Food Chemistry, British scientists report finding compounds known as kukoamines in potatoes. These compounds have been previously found only in herbal medicine from a plant (Lycium chinense), the bark of which is used in Chinese medicine to make a tea for lowering BP. However, more investigation is needed to find out if they are stable during cooking.

Japanese researchers reported in 2004 that drinking fermented milk daily can reduce BP in hypertensive men. The fermented milk in question (made by Calpis) contains two tripeptides that have been shown to lower BP, probably by inhibiting angiotensin-converting enzyme (ACE) but without the side effects of that class of antihypertensive drugs.

In most cases, therefore, diet and exercise can lower blood pressure.

If this austere regime is getting you down, you could always eat some dark chocolate to cheer you up! Eating dark chocolate every day for two weeks not only lowers BP but also reduces the risk of diabetes, claims an article published in a 2005 issue of the American Journal of Clinical Nutrition. This is due to the presence of antioxidants called flavonoids that are found not only in cocoa but also in the seeds and skins of fruits, in red wine and in tea. White chocolate, which contains no cocoa, has no flavonoid and showed no such effect.

When all else fails, medications such as diuretics, beta-blockers, calcium channel blockers or ACE inhibitors are called for. Unfortunately, these can have some undesirable side effects!

A TASTE OF HONEY

Honey has been used as a food and a sweetener for at least 8,000 years. Its use for medicinal purposes is almost as old, having been mentioned in many ancient texts, including the Old and the New Testaments.

Honey is made by honeybees from the nectar that they collect from flowers. The nectar is stored in the bee's 'honey sack' which may require stopping at more than 1,000 flowers to fill up. Back at the hive, other worker bees suck up the nectar into their mouths where enzymes break down the complex sugars into simpler ones, which are easier for the bees to digest. The nectar is then dispersed around the honeycombs, causing the water to evaporate which results in the syrup becoming thicker. When the honey is thick enough and has filled each cell of the honeycomb, it is then plugged with wax. The honey remains in storage until the bees need it for food, usually in winter.

Honey consists of almost equal amounts of two sugars, fructose (38.5%) and glucose (31%) together with water (17%), some complex sugars, enzymes, organic acids, vitamins and minerals. Thanks to its high fructose content, honey tastes twice as sweet as ordinary sugar. The vitamins include vitamin C, vitamin B6, niacin, riboflavin and pantothenic acid while calcium, magnesium, phosphorus, potassium and zinc are some of the minerals that are found in honey.

Honey also contains several antioxidants of the flavonoid

type including pinocembrin, quercetin and luteolin. The darker the honey, the higher the antioxidant level. Since bees collect nectar from many varieties of flowers, honey will obviously vary in taste, colour and antioxidant capacity depending on the floral source. The colour can range from almost colourless to dark brown while the taste can vary from mild to strong. Honey from alfalfa and clover is light in colour and mild tasting while that from buckwheat is dark and has a strong flavour.

The antioxidant capacity of honey is in the same range as that of many fruits and vegetables such as apples, oranges and spinach. Since antioxidants can reduce damage due to free radicals, which may lead to heart disease, for example, honey could be expected to offer some protection. Studies carried out at the University of Illinois at Urbana-Champaign have indeed shown that honey is quite effective at inhibiting lipoprotein oxidation by oxygen free radicals. Men who were given a mixture of honey and water daily improved their blood antioxidant levels after just five weeks. Research is now underway to see if honey will actually reduce hardening of the arteries. Incidentally, the antioxidant power of honey wine or mead is similar to that of white wine but much less than that of red wine.

The use of honey as a preservative to replace synthetic antioxidants in prepared foods such as salad dressing is also being investigated.

Honey has been used as an antiseptic for treating wounds since the early days of the ancient civilizations of Asia and the Mediterranean area. Recent research has confirmed that honey is indeed effective against common pathogens that cause infections in wounds. A honey wound dressing called Medihoney was approved for use in Australia in 1999 and a plaster containing pure honey has been in use in the

Netherlands since 2001. Honey is even being investigated as a potential alternative to combat strains of bacteria that have become resistant to commonly used antibiotics.

Many factors account for the antimicrobial properties of honey such as its low water content and relatively high acidity, which are not conducive to the growth of bacteria and yeasts. Honey tends to remove water from bacteria through the process of osmosis, thus causing the bacteria to die.

Of the many enzymes that honey contains, glucose oxidase is of particular interest since it reacts with glucose to form hydrogen peroxide, a well-known disinfectant. However, light, and especially heat from pasteurization, will reduce the peroxide antimicrobial effect. Other factors, such as the presence of organic acids, may also contribute to the antibacterial effect of honey and are not affected by pasteurization.

Honey has also been used for centuries as a beauty product. Cleopatra is reputed to have taken milk and honey baths. Honey has been added to skin moisturizers since it attracts and retains moisture in the skin.

Despite its image as a wholesome and natural food, some types of honey may contain small quantities of pyrrolizidine alkaloids, potent plant poisons that are found in about 3% of flowering plants, according to the Journal of Agricultural and Food Chemistry. Tansy ragwort (Senecio jacobaea), comfrey (Symphytum officinale) and borage (Borago officinalis) are some of the common plants producing these alkaloids. It is particularly worrisome that borage cultivation is spreading in Europe after borage oil was found to be high in a heart-healthy omega-3 fatty acid.

Other bee products such as bee propolis, pollen and royal jelly have been touted as a cure for arthritis and cancer. Royal jelly is the food for bee larvae while propolis is a resin which bees mix with wax for caulking their honeycomb. Propolis is rich in flavonoids and organic acids such as caffeic acid, which may account for its antibacterial properties. Anecdotal accounts on its effectiveness abound but scientific evidence is slim at present.

A Chinese study found that extracts of propolis were active against Staphylococcus aureus bacteria, which are responsible for infections and blood poisoning while a Japanese study presented evidence for the effectiveness of royal jelly against gram-positive bacteria. In addition to their antibacterial effect, bee products have been found to slow down the growth and spread of cancer cells in mice, according to a 2004 study carried out at the University of Zagreb. However, more research is needed to confirm the above results.

So, honey may be a good alternative to sugar as a sweetener. Some studies have also found that honey could even kill the bacteria responsible for tooth decay! If you have a sweet tooth, this is the kind of news you like to hear!

HOW TO LOSE WEIGHT...WITHOUT REALLY GOING ON A DIET!

The beginning of a new year is often the time when people think about dieting, some to lose the extra pounds they put on during the festivities and others to craft a new body image. Naturally, many turn to popular diet plans such as Weight Watchers, Pritikin, Atkins, the Zone and South Beach. These plans rely on consuming smaller portions (Weight Watchers), limiting intake of fats (Pritikin) or carbohydrates (Atkins) or a combination of these three (South Beach, the Zone).

Lately, the most popular diet plans have been those that call for a drastic reduction in carbohydrate consumption while allowing almost unlimited access to protein and fats. These plans are based on the premise that when carbohydrates, which include the sugars, starches, gums and cellulose that are found in vegetables, fruits and whole grains, are eaten, the insulin that is released not only causes an increase in the appetite but also allows the body to store more fat. With a high fat or protein diet, the body would switch from burning glucose, which it normally gets from the digestion of carbohydrates, to burning stored fat for energy thus resulting in weight loss. So, in essence by cutting out carbohydrates and replacing them with protein and fat, you would lose weight. However, a recent article in the 'Journal of the American Medical Association', analyzing many of the low carbohydrate diets, did not find enough evidence to justify their effectiveness or safety. Only those who stayed on the diet and consumed fewer calories over an extended period had a significant weight loss.

The concern with these high fat, high protein and low carbohydrate diets is that intake of vegetables, whole grains and fruits are limited, so minerals, vitamins and fibre may be lacking. This is also true to some extent for other calorie restricted diets. There is an initial weight loss but it's due mostly to the loss of fluids. If there is further weight loss, it's mainly due to taking in less calories. However, over the long term the high protein and fat diet could affect kidney function, increase cholesterol and the risk of heart disease, cancer, especially colon cancer, and osteoporosis.

A study of the Atkins diet published in the 'New England Journal of Medicine' did find that people on it for six months lose more weight than those on other low calorie diets. However, after one year there was almost no difference. Another surprising finding was that one-third to one half of the participants drop out within a year and return to their old habits, thus gaining all the weight they had lost. And this despite the fact that the Atkins diet allows you to eat your fill of high fat foods which, of course, will not make you get as hungry as people who are on low calorie diets!

So, what should you do? Well, if you do not want to gain weight, the number of calories from the food you eat must be equal to the calories that you burn through the normal body processes and through exercise. If you want to lose weight, you have to safely reduce some of the calories from food without compromising your intake of nutrients and increase the amount of exercise. This may involve a lifestyle change so that you can maintain your weight over the long term. A crash diet is definitely not the way to go!

So, choose a diet that suits you and will make you lose weight gradually without making you feel weak or dehydrated, as will be the case when stored body fat is metabolized rapidly. Do not make big changes to your eating habits and your attitude regarding food and exercise, since these will be too stressful for you to handle in the long run. Instead make small and gradual changes in your eating patterns. For example, instead of eating four pieces of toast for breakfast, eat only three. Serve your main meal in a smaller plate in order to reduce portion size while still keeping the plate full.

The most important thing to do is to eat when you are hungry. Do not let any diet plan make you feel starved, for then you'll overeat the next chance you get. Eat regularly and make sure you have small amounts of protein and at least five portions of fruits and vegetables, together with plenty of whole grains. These are generally low in calories, especially if you do not add butter or rich sauces to them, are high in nutrients and are filling too. You also need some good fats such as the omega-3 fatty acids from oily fish and monounsaturated fats from olive and canola oils. Eat low fat cheeses and drink skim milk. Don't ban desserts but eat them occasionally and you won't feel deprived. However, do not snack in between meals on chips, cookies, chocolate bars, ice cream or crackers.

The other key factor in keeping your weight stable is exercise and staying active. Exercise burns off fat and builds lean muscles, which then burn more calories than fat does, even if you do not exercise!

And stay away from high protein diets, especially if you are trying to get pregnant. Animal studies at the Colorado Centre for Reproductive Medicine have shown that protein-rich diets lower fertility!

PEANUTS AND PEANUT BUTTER: IT'S NOT NUTS TO EAT THEM!

Peanuts (Arachis hypogea) belong to the same legume family as peas and beans, despite being formed underground. They are thought to have originated in South America over 5,000 years ago. The Spaniards brought them to Asia while the Portuguese introduced them to Africa, and from there they were brought to the USA. Many species exist today including the small, round Spanish peanuts, the medium Valencia ones and the larger Virginia peanuts.

Peanuts are a nutritious and healthy addition to anyone's diet despite their high fat content (about 20% by weight). Most of it, though, is of the good variety. 85% of the fat in peanuts is unsaturated with 60% of that being monounsaturated and about 30% polyunsaturated, of which a small amount is of the omega-3 type.

You are not going nuts if you think that eating peanuts is a way of controlling obesity! In fact, research shows you can eat peanuts and even lose weight! Despite their high fat content and calories, several studies have shown that consumption of a handful of peanuts daily for six months did not result in an increase in weight. This is due to the high protein and fibre content, which will keep you feeling full longer. In fact, a study done at Purdue University showed that people who ate nuts everyday did not increase their overall calorie intake since they ate less at other times. By substituting peanuts for snacks containing saturated fats or refined carbohydrates, people will not put on weight. However, stay away from salted peanuts, as they are loaded with salt which most of us consume too much of already.

Despite the strong evidence that consuming peanuts regularly can help you lose weight, there is still some reluctance to follow suit because of their high fat content. However, moderate consumption of good fats, such as the monounsaturated fats found in peanuts, olive or canola oil and avocado, is better than a typical, low fat diet for losing weight and for heart health.

According to a paper in Neurology published in 2005, a diet rich in mono and polyunsaturated fatty acids lowers the risk of Parkinson's disease. This could possibly be another benefit of eating peanuts.

Peanuts are high in good quality protein, about 25 grams per 100 grams of peanuts, which is more than any other nut. As the level of some essential amino acids is somewhat low in peanuts, by combining a peanut butter sandwich with a glass of milk, you top up the low amino acids and have a complete protein food.

A small percentage of the population (about 1%) suffers from food allergies, especially from peanuts and other nuts, which often are mild but can sometimes be life threatening due to anaphylactic shock. Signs of allergic reactions can include swelling in the mouth, difficulty breathing, stomach problems, skin rash, rapid pulse rate, drop in blood pressure and dizziness which can result in the person becoming unconscious. People who suspect that they may be allergic to nuts should start an elimination diet to see if they really are. Common allergens such as peanuts can then be eliminated from the diet. Similarly, people afflicted with eczema, which is often linked to allergies, should avoid foods considered to be high in allergens, such as peanuts.

Peanuts are also rich in vitamin E, folate, niacin, potassium, zinc, phytosterols and antioxidants, all of which are important to our health. University of Florida researchers have found that peanuts are high in antioxidants known as polyphenols, almost as high as fruits and berries. One such polyphenol is p-coumaric acid and its level, in fact, is increased when peanuts are roasted.

Incidentally, if you like roasted peanuts, buy dry-roasted instead of oil-roasted ones since the latter add unnecessary calories from fat, which could include saturated ones such as coconut oil. Once peanuts have been roasted, the fats in them will oxidize rapidly which will lead to rancidity.

Trans-resveratrol, another polyphenol found in peanuts, is also found in red wine. An ounce of peanuts has about half the trans-resveratrol content of a fluid ounce of red wine. Trans-resveratrol protects against oxidation of 'bad' LDL cholesterol in the blood, thus preventing the formation of arterial plaques, which can lead to stroke and heart attacks.

In addition, one ounce of peanuts provides about 10% each of our daily requirements of vitamin E and folic acid, both of which can help reduce the risk of heart disease.

Diabetics also benefit from eating peanuts and most other nuts since the body digests them slowly, thus avoiding the rapid increase in blood insulin level that normally occurs after eating carbohydrate-rich foods.

Research in the Department of Physical Therapy, Exercise and Nutrition Sciences of State University of New York at Buffalo showed that peanuts are also rich in beta-sitosterol, which has been shown to protect against some cancers such as those of the colon, breast and prostate. This effect is probably magnified by the presence of antioxidants in peanuts.

So, who says all candies are bad for you? Not if they contain peanuts! A two-ounce bar of Snickers, for example, containing about 23 peanuts, may be good not only for your palate but also for your health!

About half of the peanuts harvested in the US are converted into peanut butter, which was first introduced at the St. Louis World Fair in 1904. There are many types of peanut butter, smooth, crunchy, those made with only peanuts and others made with added hydrogenated oils, starch or other additives. You should avoid brands of peanut butter in which the fat content has been lowered by the addition of flour, sugar or other fillers since these will reduce the health benefits.

Some peanut butter contains added hydrogenated peanut oil to solidify it, thus preventing any oil from rising to the top. During the hydrogenation process, harmful trans fatty acids are formed although admittedly their levels tend to be low, less than 0.2% or 0.05 g per serving of 32 g. Some confusion may arise as a result of new labelling regulations, which may indicate there is no trans fat even though hydrogenated oil is listed as a stabilizer! According to new FDA guidelines, foods containing less than 0.5g per serving would be listed as having no trans fats! If you want to stay clear of any trans fats, choose natural or organic peanut butter.

Furthermore, a paper from the Faculty of Pharmacy of Barcelona University, published in the Journal of Agriculture and Food Chemistry, showed that the antioxidant trans-resveratrol and its glucoside, trans-piceid, are present in higher amounts in natural peanut butters than in blended ones.

Peanut butter should be kept in the fridge to prevent it going rancid. Peanuts that have gone mouldy should not be eaten as they may contain aflatoxins, which have been shown to be carcinogens in animal studies. One of the most toxic of the aflatoxins, aflatoxin B1, can cause cancer in humans, in particular cancer of the liver.

Peanuts, peanut butter and nuts in general, have been found to be good for the heart if they are consumed in moderation—about two tablespoons per serving. They contain monounsaturated fatty acids such as oleic acid and an omega-3-fatty acid, linolenic acid, that have been shown to protect the heart by lowering the 'bad' LDL cholesterol and total cholesterol levels. This could also be due to many of the other constituents of peanuts including folate, fibre, magnesium, potassium, copper, selenium, vitamin E, resveratrol, phytosterols and arginine.

Population studies, such as the Adventists Health Study, the Iowa Women's Health Study and the Physicians' Health Study, have shown that regular consumption of peanuts, peanut butter and nuts reduces the risk of coronary heart disease by 25-50% even for those individuals who are in their early eighties!

A 1998 paper in the British Medical Journal from the Harvard School of Public Health, Harvard Medical School and Brigham and Women's Hospital found that in the Nurses' Health Study of 86,016 women, after adjusting for known risk factors of coronary heart disease and making allowances for consumption of heart-healthy dietary fats, fruits and vegetables, those individuals consuming one serving of peanuts (1 ounce or 28 grams) or other nuts more than five times a week, had a reduced risk of heart disease compared to those who didn't eat nuts.

Another study from the Graduate Program in Nutrition of Pennsylvania State University and the Department of Community and Preventive Medicine of the University of Rochester Medical Centre, published in the American Journal of Clinical Nutrition in 1999, found that a diet high in peanut oil reduced coronary heart disease risk by 16%.

In addition to reducing heart disease risks, peanuts can also keep type-2 diabetes at bay. A 2002 epidemiological study based on the Nurses' Health Study from the Harvard School of Public Health and the Brigham and Women's Hospital, published in the Journal of the American Medical Association, found that one ounce of peanuts or other nuts, or a tablespoon of peanut butter consumed daily, reduced the risk of getting type-2 diabetes by 21-25%. A higher intake enhanced proportionately the protective effect!

It is thought that this protection is due to the unsaturated fatty acids as well as fibre and magnesium, which have been found to decrease insulin resistance thus reducing the risk of type-2 diabetes.

By eating foods that will break down into glucose slowly, such as peanuts, the risk of diabetes is reduced. According to the Harvard team, there may be other factors in peanuts that play a role in reducing type-2 diabetes since the apparent benefit is more than can be explained by the fat, fibre and magnesium that they contain.

People with a peanut allergy are the only ones that have to stay away from peanuts while others may have to watch the amount they consume. For example, peanuts are rich in oxalate so people who have a tendency to form kidney stones should be careful about their peanut consumption.

It has also been found that the cold sore virus (Herpes simplex) requires high levels of the amino acid arginine to flourish while another amino acid, lysine stops it from replicating. People with a tendency to develop cold sores, therefore, should cut back on arginine-rich foods, such as peanuts, and increase instead their lysine intake.

For the rest of us, we can go nuts on peanuts!

PROSTATE CANCER: DIET CAN HELP
REDUCE THE RISK

The walnut-sized prostate, whose main role is to produce semen, is a gland located between the bladder and the rectum. Men over the age of 40 have an increasing risk of getting an enlarged prostate, which could eventually become cancerous. There are several risk factors associated with prostate cancer, such as age, race, lifestyle and diet, some of which can be modified.

Prostate cancer can be cured, especially if caught early and this is why a yearly check-up with a digital rectal examination and a prostate-specific antigen (PSA) test is recommended. PSA, a protein made in the prostate, helps keep the semen fluid. Despite its name, PSA is also produced by women!

Many conditions, apart from prostate cancer, can lead to an elevated PSA reading, such as a benign, enlarged prostate, infections of the prostate or the lower urinary tract as well as ejaculation 24 hours before the test. A PSA level of 0 to 3.9 nanograms per ml of blood is considered normal in most cases. Since prostate cancer develops slowly, men who are over 75 need not do the test since they are more likely to die of something else.

Diet, especially a high-fat one with plenty of red meat, seems to play a part in the development of the disease. Harvard researchers reported as early as 1993 that men who consumed red meat most often had twice the risk of prostate cancer compared to those who ate it less often. Red meat was defined as beef, veal, lamb or pork. It is thought that the high temperatures needed to cook the meat produce cancer-causing compounds, such as heterocyclic amines, which increase the risk.

Since prostate cancer usually develops slowly, changes in the diet must be initiated early for it to work. To be effective, men should reduce their intake of red meat and other food containing saturated, animal fat or trans fats such as dairy products, cookies, doughnuts and French fries. Instead, consumption of whole grains, fruits and vegetables should be increased and a normal weight maintained by exercising regularly.

Countries where a lot of fat is consumed, such as the U.K, have high levels of prostate cancer as well as heart disease. Fat may be the culprit but surprisingly, so could calcium from the high-fat dairy products. It appears that too much calcium lowers the active form of vitamin D in the blood. However, to get too much calcium one must consume over 2,000 mg per day, which would be quite a feat in a normal diet!

Vitamin D which, in adequate amounts, is thought to protect the prostate, is obtained from the reaction of the sun's UVB rays on the skin and also from fortified milk and cereals, oily fish and eggs.

A study from the Medical School of the University of Tampere, Finland, published in the January 2004 issue of the International Journal of Cancer, identified both low and high blood levels of vitamin D as being linked to higher risks of prostate cancer.

Race is also a factor in the risk of getting the disease with blacks having the highest, followed by whites and Asians who have the lowest. Previous studies have linked levels of testosterone in men with prostate cancer risk. For example, a meta-analysis in the Journal of Clinical Oncology from Harvard Medical School and Harvard School of Public Health concluded that men having testosterone in the upper quartile of the population have twice the risk of getting prostate cancer.

However, Asians migrating to North America catch up with the higher local rate, showing that environment and diet also have a profound influence on the disease. An article in a National Cancer Institute monogram by T. Hirayama considers the possibility of a lack of vitamin A, from inadequate consumption of green and yellow vegetables in North America, as being the culprit.

Several studies have shown the benefit of antioxidants such as selenium, vitamin E, vitamin A, lycopene and other carotenoids in preventing prostate cancer by reducing oxidative stress. The latter, according to a paper in Cancer Metastasis Review from the Sunnybrook Regional Cancer Centre of the University of Toronto, generates reactive oxygen species, which can lead to cancer.

Epidemiological studies have shown that selenium may protect against prostate cancer. For example, a 2003 paper in the International Journal of Cancer by T.M. Vogt of the National Cancer Institute of Bethesda, USA, suggests that there is a moderate reduction in the risk of prostate cancer in people with higher blood selenium concentrations.

When 200 micrograms of selenium (or a placebo) was given daily to 1,300 men whose diet was low in selenium, a reduction in prostate cancer, as well as cancers of the lung and colon, was observed. A large study by the National Cancer Institute, the 10-year Selenium and Vitamin E Cancer Trial (SELECT) with selenium and vitamin E is being conducted to see if it would reduce prostate cancer risk in healthy individuals.

However, the result will only be known in 2013. Selenium is found in Brazil nuts, turkey, fish and lentils.

Studies in Finland have also shown that four years of treatment with vitamin E (alpha-tocopherol) reduces the incidence of prostate cancer by 33% and the death rate from the disease by 41%. However, it now appears that another vitamin E isomer, gamma-tocopherol, may also be involved—although the evidence is not definite. So, people taking vitamin E supplement in order to reduce the risk of cancer may be wasting their money since it contains only alpha-tocopherol. Natural vitamin E, which occurs in nuts and oils, with all its isomers, may be more effective.

Eating tomato sauce two to four times weekly seems to be beneficial since men who did so had a 34% reduced risk compared to those who ate none. This was attributed to lycopene, a potent antioxidant that neutralizes free radicals and which also occurs naturally in the prostate. Free radicals can damage tissues and DNA, thus leading to cancer and other diseases.

According to a meta-analysis carried out by M. Etminan at the Royal Victoria Hospital of McGill University, however, it seems that to get any real benefit one must consume a very large amount of tomato sauce.

Even though we do not have definitive proof that lycopene does work, and its effect may be modest at best, it may be prudent to increase one's intake of tomato products, especially ketchup which has been found to be better absorbed by the body.

Soy, which acts as a phytoestrogen, may also be a promising addition to the prostate cancer prevention diet. After all, in Asia where soy is consumed regularly at the rate of about 10g of soy protein per day, the prostate cancer rate is low. A Journal of Nutrition article in 2000 from the University of Helsinki pinpoints phytoestrogens in the Japanese diet as being responsible for reducing the risk of prostate cancer. Joanne Davis reported in the Nutrition and Cancer Journal in 1999, that increasing consumption of soy reduced the risk of getting and dying from prostate cancer.

Soy is rich in isoflavonoids, such as genistein, which have been shown in the laboratory, but not yet in humans, to inhibit the growth of prostate cancer cells. Since isoflavonoids are weakly estrogenic it is not surprising that they inhibit the growth of prostate cells, which require male sex hormones.

Other foods that have similar properties are flaxseeds and lentils, both of which contain estrogenic lignans. Epidemiological and animal studies have indicated that a low-fat diet, together with fish oils, prevents the development of prostate cancer. For example, men consuming fish, such as salmon or tuna, two to four times weekly had a lower rate of prostate cancer than those eating it less often.

In addition to the vitamins A, C and E that one gets from vegetables, grains and fruits, other antioxidants, such as the polyphenols, flavonoids and anthocyanins that occur in green tea, red wine and strong onions, may be useful in lowering the risk of prostate cancer.

Can COX 2 inhibitors prevent prostate cancer? Some studies have shown that there are fewer cases of prostate cancer among men who take aspirin or ibuprofen on a regular basis. Their long-term use, however, may result in harmful side effects, especially on the liver and kidney. Curcumin, which is the active ingredient in turmeric, is a natural anti-COX 2 agent. Studies by T. Dorai at Columbia University, published in the journal Prostate in 2001, have shown that curcumin inhibits prostate cell growth. Of course, there is no long-term risk associated with turmeric since, as a major component of curry powder, it has been safely consumed in India and elsewhere for thousands of years.

According to research carried out by J. W. Chiao and co-workers at the Department of Medicine of New York Medical College, sulforaphane from cruciferous vegetables was found, in the laboratory, to stop the growth of prostate cancer cells. So, it may be wise to include cabbage, cauliflower, broccoli and kale in the diet.

However, one must not get too carried away with diet and forget about the value of exercise as a way to prevent disease. Studies at the National Cancer Institute in Bethesda and at the National Public Health Institute in Helsinki have clearly shown the protective effect of physical activity on prostate cancer risk.

So, to reduce your risk of getting prostate problems, cut down on red meat, full-fat dairy products and other foods with animal fat. Eat a lot of fruits and vegetables, more fatty fish, tomato sauce, curries, soy and have some corn, soy or sesame oil which contains gamma-tocopherol as well as vitamin E. And don't forget to drink more green tea and a daily glass of red wine.

Even if it does not completely protect against prostate cancer, the above diet, together with more exercise, will be beneficial for the heart and cancer prevention in general.

Perhaps surprisingly, recent studies have found that frequent ejaculation, through sexual intercourse or otherwise, could offer some protection against prostate cancer. However, if you want to be absolutely certain of not ever getting prostate cancer, there is only one choice—get castrated!

SALMON: WILD ABOUT SALMON!

Despite the real environmental concerns that many have, consumers in Europe and North America are now buying more farm-raised salmon than wild salmon, mainly because of price and year-round availability.

The farms, actually fish pens located in the sea close to land, supply more fresh salmon than the annual wild salmon harvest.

Salmon farming started in Norway in the 1970's. Today, the biggest producers of farmed salmon are Chile, Canada, Britain, the USA and Norway.

Farmed salmon are usually of the Atlantic salmon species because they convert feed to flesh efficiently and can be harvested in three to four years. This is why they cost about one third of the price of wild salmon.

The feed normally consists of pellets made with soy, corn, canola oil as well as fish meal and oils derived from anchovies or mackerel. Fish meal made with fish caught in the Atlantic has been found to contain trace amounts of carcinogenic contaminants such as dioxins and polychlorinated biphenyls (PCB) and polybrominated diphenyl ethers (PBDE). PCBs were used as coolants and lubricants in transformers and, although banned more than twenty years ago, they still persist in the environment. More recently chemical flame retardants, PBDEs, have also been found in fish meal, according to a paper published in the American Journal of Environmental Science and Technology of August, 2004.

A study on PBDEs in the US found varying levels in most food of animal origin, such as meat, fish and dairy, if the fat is not removed. Even vegans in England have been shown to ingest PBDEs from their food but at only 30% of that of an omnivorous diet.

Pacific fish meal, which Canadian fish farms are increasingly turning to, appears to have less of these contaminants which, in any case, fall within the standards set by the World Health Organization. Colorants such as the carotenoids, canthaxanthin and astaxanthin, are also added to the feed so that the flesh may turn pink. Wild salmon get these pigments from the algae, crustaceans and plankton that they feed on.

Salmon is low in saturated fats and has high quality protein in addition to several nutrients such as vitamin D, zinc and selenium.

The health benefits derived from eating salmon and its omega-3 fatty acids, which are known to decrease cardiovascular disease, must be weighed against the small exposure to contaminants such as dioxins, PCBs and PBDEs.

Salmon contains two omega-3 fatty acids, docosahexaenoic acid (DHA) and eicosapentaenoic acid (EPA), which have been shown to protect against cardiovascular disease and several cancers. Eating salmon once or twice a week is enough to help protect against heart disease. Wild Pacific salmon is, of course, preferable since they do not have residues of antibiotics or pesticides although they may have some mercury. Wild fish in general have less contaminants since they feed on much smaller fish, shrimp and krill. Unlike their wild counterparts, farmed salmon are generally bigger and fattier. Farmed salmon contain more PCBs since these are stored in their fat and stay there for a long time. To reduce the contaminant level in cooked salmon, one has to lower the amount of fat in it by removing the skin before cooking, and broiling or grilling it rather than poaching.

Salmon is not the only source of omega-3 fatty acids. These are also found in many other wild fish as well as in canola and flaxseed oils and soy.

Pregnant and nursing women need DHA, which is vital for the proper development of the baby's brain and retina. However, they should eat canned or wild salmon or smaller fish such as sardines or mackerel, which have far less contaminants than bigger ones. DHA is not only essential for the growth and functional development of the brain in infants but also for maintenance of normal brain function in adults.

The mechanism by which omega-3 fatty acids protect against heart disease, oxidative stress, depression, arthritis and other inflammatory diseases is slowly becoming clear. For example, in a 2004 issue of the Journal of Experimental Medicine, scientists have discovered that omega-3 fatty acids are broken down into a new class of fatty acids called resolvins. Scientists found that resolvin E1 helps reduce the immune response and the development of serious diseases by stopping certain immune cells from going to inflammation sites. They have shown that people who ate foods rich in omega-3 fatty acids, as well as those who took a low-dose aspirin regularly, had some resolvin E1 in their blood.

The risks of regularly consuming farmed salmon, on the other hand, have also been well documented. An Indiana University study published in a 2004 issue of Science found the farmed fish contain more PCBs than wild ones, with the most contaminated fish coming from Scotland and the Faroe Islands. Farmed fish have been found to contain ten times more PCB and four times more PBDE than wild ones, although the actual numbers are well within the accepted Health Canada and WHO limits, but not the US Environmental Protection Agency's. The average level of PCB in salmon was found to be 0.027 parts per million (ppm) whereas the current Health Canada limit is 2 ppm. In fact, Health Canada came flat out and declared that the levels of these two pollutants are very low and do not pose a risk.

It is noteworthy that PCBs are also found in many other foods that we consume such as beef, pork and lamb.

There is no doubt that PCBs and PBDEs can increase the risk of getting cancer, especially cancer of the liver, but from the available information on farmed salmon, this risk is small, though not negligible.

So, what should the health-conscious person do? Well, you have to weigh the benefits of eating farm-raised salmon against the risks! Chances are you will be better off eating salmon, especially if you are an older person!

As you get older, the risk of getting a heart attack or stroke is much higher than that of getting cancer, which may take years to develop. The American Heart Association, in fact, recommends that people without any sign of heart disease eat fatty fish like salmon twice a week. Those with heart disease should eat even more; however, the Federal Drug Agency has determined that, at present, the scientific evidence to support this advice is not conclusive.

How can we sum up this debate? Eating salmon regularly could increase your risk of getting cancer slightly in the long run but, at the same time, it is more likely to help you live longer by cutting down your chances of getting a heart attack!

SELENIUM: CAN THIS TRACE MINERAL PREVENT CANCER?

Selenium was first discovered by the Swedish chemist Berzelius in 1817 and named after the Greek moon goddess, Selene. However, it was only in 1957 that it was found to be an essential trace element in the diet of mammals and birds.

It is present in soil although some areas of the world, such as parts of China, are deficient in it. Modern intensive farming is reducing the selenium content of food since the small amounts released in the soil every year must be shared by many more plants. Mandatory soil enrichment with selenium in Finland has led to a significant decrease in cancer mortality, especially the types of cancer prevalent in areas deficient in the mineral.

Selenium is vital to our health since it is not only an antioxidant but is also involved in thyroid hormone metabolism, proper functioning of the immune system and protection against cancer. Many studies have shown a link between the intake of selenium and a reduced cancer risk.

How could selenium protect against cancer? Many mechanisms have been proposed including repairing DNA when needed, stopping the spread of cancer cells by increased immune system activity and restoring the 'suicide switch' in damaged cells (apoptosis).

Selenium is an essential part of several enzymes including glutathione peroxidase, which is a potent antioxidant protecting cell membranes against free radicals, and may thus help reduce the risk of developing not only cancer but also heart disease, arthritis and viral diseases. Research has shown that glutathione peroxidase is used in the liver to neutralise reactive chemical species which may be dangerous to our health. If the level of this enzyme is low, these species may damage cells and their DNA, thus initiating the development of cancer.

Selenium is found in small amounts in most foods but especially in organ meats, egg yolks, mushrooms, nuts, whole grains, dairy products, garlic, fish and seafood in general. Research carried out in the Netherlands and in the U.K has shown that absorption of selenium from fish is as effective as that from plant foods. The processing of fish by cooking or salting, did not affect the bioavailability of selenium. Brazil nuts are also rich in selenium and a couple of them, freshly shelled, meet our daily adult requirement of up to 200 micrograms for this mineral. It is interesting to note that packaged, shelled Brazil nuts contain less than a quarter of the selenium content of the unshelled ones.

In general, foods that are rich in protein will also contain selenium. For example, four slices of roast turkey (about 100 grams) supply nearly half of our daily requirement of this mineral.

Since selenium and sulfur have similar chemical properties, foods that contain sulfur such as garlic, onion and leek will also have a fair amount of selenium. However, there is a geographical variation in selenium intake because of the bioavailability of the element which, for example, is generally low in Europe.

In fact, concern has been expressed in the U.K about the falling level of selenium in the diet, which is partly due to lower imports of wheat from the selenium-rich prairies of Canada and the US. A study published in the Journal of the Science of Food and Agriculture showed that wheat used for making bread in England contains 10 to 50 times less selenium than the corresponding grains in Canada and the US. Even in the US, the Agricultural Research Service of the US Department of Agriculture is investigating the potential benefits of fortifying flour with selenium.

Taking selenium in pill form is not advisable as it would be easy to consume an excessive amount, which could then lead to intestinal problems, nerve damage, hair loss and other signs of selenium toxicity. This is because there is a fine line between the therapeutic and toxic levels of selenium, unlike most other minerals. However, children suffering from Keshan disease, a heart ailment caused by a deficiency in dietary selenium in parts of China, have been successfully treated by supplementing their diet with selenium.

Vegetables such as garlic and broccoli store selenium as selenium methyl selenocysteine (SeMSC) whereas in grains and meat, it is found as selenomethionine. Research on the anticancer property of selenium indicates that the active species is methyl selenol, which is easily formed in one step from SeMSC by breaking off the cysteine moiety during its metabolism by the body. Selenomethionine, on the other hand, is converted to methyl selenol after several long steps, which means that it may not be as effective as SeMSC in preventing cancer. In addition, it appears that selenium works better as an antioxidant when it is combined with vitamin E. In fact, the Selenium and Vitamin E Cancer Prevention Trial (SELECT) is in the process of studying the impact these two nutrients have on prostate cancer.

Evidence is accruing from both animal and human studies that there is an increased risk of getting cancer as a result of too low concentrations of selenium in the diet. For example, when a cancer-causing compound was added to the diet of laboratory rats after they had been fed selenium-enriched mushrooms for two weeks, they had only half of the DNA damage compared to rats given regular mushrooms or a normal diet.

In a study carried out in 2003 at Purdue University, and published in the Journal of the National Cancer Institute, elderly dogs fed a diet that was supplemented with selenium had less damage done to the DNA in their prostates, compared to those that were given a normal diet. The researchers concluded that selenium could benefit ageing prostates by reducing the damage done to the cells' DNA even before they become cancerous.

Epidemiological studies carried out at Stanford University and published in the Journal of Urology in 2001 found that men who had high blood levels of selenium had a reduced risk of getting prostate cancer. Other studies have found that even among people who have sufficient levels of selenium in their diet, those who have higher blood levels are less likely to have cancer.

A double-blind study of over one thousand older patients with skin cancer at the University of Arizona by Dr L. Clark, showed that an intake of 200 micrograms of selenium daily reduced the risk of getting prostate cancer by 69%, colon cancer by 64% and lung cancer by 39%! However, it did not prevent the recurrence of skin cancer. A new study is now being planned in order to see if selenium is also effective in reducing breast and ovarian cancers.

A study published by the National Cancer Institute, found that men who consumed the most selenium in their diet had 65% less cases of advanced prostate cancer compared to those that had the lowest intake of selenium. What is different in this research is that the level of selenium was determined by an analysis of toe clippings, which reflects the intake of selenium over a long period of time.

A much larger study called PRECISE, Prevention of Cancer with Selenium in Europe and America, is now underway to see if selenium can indeed reduce the cancer risk in healthy individuals.

According to research done at Maastricht University in Holland, a high level of selenium in the diet tends to halve the risk of smokers getting bladder cancer, which is linked to cigarette smoking and environmental pollutants in general. However, it had no effect on non-smokers. According to the scientists, this shows that the antioxidant activity of selenium is responsible for this action since it works only in cases where the oxidative stress is high, such as in long-term smokers.

Research on the effect of selenium on colorectal cancer has yielded mixed results. However, an epidemiological study published in November 2004, in the Journal of the National Cancer Institute found an association between higher blood levels of selenium and reduced rates of colorectal cancer.

In addition to protecting against cancer, dietary selenium could also keep viruses in check. A recent study on mice at the US department of Agriculture has found evidence that a deficiency in selenium in the diet could help the spread of different viruses in the body, such as those responsible for the common cold and AIDS. In fact, recent research indicates that when mice deficient in selenium are infected with the human influenza virus, the latter becomes more virulent. Similarly, a clinical study at the University of Miami found that children with AIDS died at a younger age if their selenium level was low.

Increased protection against viruses may be due to a boost

in immunity afforded by selenium. In fact, a double-blind study at the University of Brussels found that elderly patients who were taking 100 micrograms of selenium daily showed marked improvement in some factors involved in the immune system. With a threatened flu pandemic on the horizon, maybe we all need to pay more attention to our consumption of selenium rich foods!

As for the link between selenium and protection against heart disease, it is rather tenuous at present. One would expect that since selenium is an antioxidant, it would inhibit the oxidation of LDL cholesterol and plaque build-up, thus reducing the risk of coronary heart disease. Some studies showed such a link although a recent study from Harvard University did not find any evidence to support it.

If all these facts about selenium are getting you down, take heart. According to research carried out in Wales, selenium appears to be needed in order to brighten one's mood! That's something from which we could all benefit!

STRONG BONES: A LIFELONG AFFAIR!

Building strong bones starts in childhood but we have to work on it for the rest of our lives to keep them strong. Our bones experience the most growth during the first three years of life. After slowing down for a few years, rapid growth resumes during adolescence, peaking at around 30. Once we have reached 35, however, instead of growing bones, we start to lose bone mass.

The bones in our body are all built around a framework of collagen on which tiny crystals of calcium from the blood are deposited so that eventually they fill up the whole surface area. Every one of the 206 bones that an adult has is made up of a hard covering layer of calcium salts, with many channels inside the bone to enable nutrients and waste materials to be ferried about. The collagen framework makes bones somewhat elastic while the calcium salts harden them.

If you want your bones to be strong when you get older, you need to build up your bone mass when you are still young. Several studies including one published in Pediatric Nursing in 1996 by AM Gallo from the College of Nursing of the University of Chicago has emphasized the need to build strong bones in childhood in order to reduce the risk of osteoporosis and skeletal fractures in later life. Osteoporosis is the disease responsible for bones becoming weak and brittle, making them more susceptible to breakage.

In order to get strong bones, as strong as your genetics

will allow you, you will need to regularly eat foods that are rich in calcium, have an adequate supply of vitamin D and do weight-bearing exercises.

An analysis of over fifty studies by R.P. Heaney from Creighton University, published in the Journal of the American College of Nutrition of 2000, confirmed that a high calcium intake promotes bone health.

The simplest way to get calcium for most people, especially children and adolescents, is from milk and milk products. Since dairy products also contain fat, the low-fat versions should be chosen. Teenagers need to be informed about their calcium needs and told that, unlike milk, soft drinks may fill them up but do not give them calcium. In fact, some carbonated drinks contain phosphates, which can increase the loss of calcium from bones. The US Institute of Medicine recommends that children aged nine to eighteen years have about 1,300 mg of calcium per day, which is about what you get in a quart of milk. For people who find it difficult to digest dairy products, hard cheeses or yoghurt may be better alternatives.

Other good sources of calcium include salmon, sardines, tofu, dried beans and green leafy vegetables such as broccoli, collards and kale. Spinach is an exception since its calcium, although abundant, is tied up with oxalic acid as water-insoluble calcium oxalate, which is not easily absorbed.

Fortified orange juice is now available for those who cannot get enough calcium from their food. As far as supplements are concerned, a good one is calcium citrate since it dissolves in the stomach easily and is also well absorbed. However, stay away from bone meal supplements since they may be contaminated with impurities such as lead.

Many studies have shown that other minerals, such as magnesium, boron, manganese and silicon, may work in conjunction with calcium to build bones.

A plateful of cooked beans of any type is a rich source of calcium supplying about 100 mg of this mineral as well as some magnesium.

Numerous studies have shown that boron and magnesium may be needed for optimal calcium metabolism, which may affect the formation and maintenance of bones. For example, a paper in Magnesium Trace Element of 1990 from the Grand Forks Human Nutrition Research Centre of the US Department of Agriculture claims that these minerals are also needed to prevent bone loss in older women and men.

Another paper published in 1993 in Progress in Food and Nutrition Science, from the Department of Biochemistry of the University of Sydney, speculates that boron, which one gets from fruits, vegetables, nuts and legumes, may increase the concentration of male and female sex hormones which are involved in calcium metabolism.

For the body to use calcium and the other minerals needed for bone synthesis, about 200 IU of vitamin D daily is necessary. Adequate vitamin D is obtained by exposing the skin to the sun for about 15 minutes per day. Older people who do not get enough sunshine, or who may lack stomach acid to process calcium from their food, may need to take a vitamin D supplement. Vitamin D is found in foods such as fish, eggs and fortified milk.

Weight-bearing exercises are also necessary, together with adequate intake of calcium, to stimulate formation of new bone tissues thus making bones become stronger, especially in adolescence, according to a 2001 article in Public Health and Nutrition from F. Branca at Rome's National Institute of Food and Nutrition. Since exercise also helps reduce calcium loss, it is not surprising to find that sedentary individuals and astronauts in the weightlessness of space are at a greater risk of losing bone mass.

A study from the University of British Columbia found that elementary school girls doing jumping exercises three times weekly had 5% more bone mass than those who did not.

Bone loss increases in women who have reached menopause as a result of decreasing estrogen levels. According to an article in the Journal of Bone Minerals Research of 1987 from Creighton University School of Medicine, the decrease in spine density and total bone calcium was 2.5 to 3 times greater in the 25 years after menopause than before, with the greatest change occurring in the first five years following menopause. So, if you had maximized calcium storage in your youth, you may not be too badly affected, especially if your calcium intake is still high and you exercise regularly. However, if you do not get adequate calcium from the diet, your body will take the calcium it needs from your bones, thus causing them to become weaker. So, you not only need to have enough calcium in the diet but you also need to keep it in your bones!

Not all nutritionists agree that milk is the best source of calcium, however, or even that it is needed for bone health. A small minority of nutritionists argues that the US has a high osteoporosis and bone fracture rate despite having the highest milk consumption. Furthermore, a 12-year Harvard study of 78,000 women, which showed that those who drank milk three times per day had more bone fractures than those who rarely drank milk. A 1994 study of the elderly in Sydney, Australia, found that those with the highest dairy consumption had double the number of hip fractures of those with the lowest intake, while a 2002 report published in Pediatrics showed that children who drank more milk do not have healthier bones.

These nutritionists argue that to build strong bones, children need to have a diet rich in vegetables and fruits, get enough daily exercise and sunshine. As for adults, they can reduce calcium losses by cutting down on salt, caffeine, tobacco and animal protein, by being physically active, and by taking vitamin D supplements if necessary.

By the way, did you know that beer is also good for your bones? It seems that the silicon in beer helps calcium and the other minerals in building stronger bones.

TURKEY: WHAT WOULD CHRISTMAS BE WITHOUT IT?

"Eat not to dullness, drink not to elevation."
These words of advice from Benjamin Franklin usually fall on deaf ears at Christmas time. However, if we do indulge in a few excesses once in a while, they can't do much harm! After all, there are many reasons for enjoying Christmas, not the least of which is the Christmas dinner.

For most people who are not vegetarians, turkey with cranberry sauce is the highlight of the dinner. The toast is made with a glass of wine, preferably red even though this may make the purists see red! Chocolate and nuts may round off the meal. We will, of course, assume that cholesterol laden or high calorie components of the meal, such as gravy, stuffing and Christmas log, are limited. Bearing in mind this proviso, the Christmas dinner can be a healthy meal. Turkey, cranberries, red wine, chocolate and nuts not only look good on a candle-lit festive table but they are also good for you.

The centerpiece for most people's table is a perfectly roasted turkey. This is easier said than done. An average turkey contains about 70% of tender, white breast meat and 30% of tougher, dark meat from the legs and wings. Why are the colours of the meat different? That's because the active muscles of the legs contain a multitude of blood vessels carrying muscle hemoglobin, also referred to as myoglobin, bringing oxygen to the muscles. The darker the meat, the more myoglobin it contains. The dark meat also contains more tough connective tissues, such as collagen, which are converted to soft gelatin on prolonged heating above 70 degrees Celsius. The white breast meat, on the other hand, contains muscles, which were originally used for flying in wild turkeys, but not used by farm-raised birds. Hence, there is no need for a lot of myoglobin, as the white meat attests.

So, how do you thoroughly cook the tougher dark meat without overcooking the tender white meat? We assume that you want to put the whole bird on the table for carving instead of bits of legs and breast that have been cooked separately!

It appears that there are several ways of doing just that. The easiest is to put an ice pack on the breast of the defrosted bird for half an hour before roasting at moderate heat, about 160 degrees Celsius, and perhaps adding 15-30 minutes to the cooking time. In this way, the breast meat will not be overdone and will stay moist while the legs and wings will be thoroughly cooked.

Or you could cover only the breast area with aluminum foil so that it does not get as hot as the legs and wings. The foil has to be removed about 15 minutes before the end of the roasting time, as indicated, preferably, by a roasting thermometer.

In some parts of the world, the stuffing is placed not in the body cavity but just under the skin, right on top of the breast meat. This slows down the cooking of the white meat while allowing the dark meat to cook faster. The stuffing has to be removed as soon as roasting is done otherwise the breast meat will continue to cook and become dry. The same thing will happen if basting of the breast is done with hot liquid from the roasting pan.

Turkey meat is high in protein and low in fat. The protein is of a high quality with all the necessary amino acids and

100g of turkey supplies about half of our daily requirement of protein.

The white meat has half of the fat found in the darker meat although both have the same amount of protein. It has also less fat than red meat and most other meat for that matter. Although touted as a healthier alternative to beef hotdogs, turkey hotdogs, in fact, have about the same high fat content as a regular hotdog.

Turkey is a good source of several important minerals such as iron, phosphorus, potassium, selenium and zinc as well as B vitamins, in particular niacin, vitamin B6 and folic acid.

Dark turkey meat has twice the amount of iron and three times more zinc than the white meat. While iron is needed to prevent anemia, zinc is vital for building a strong immune system. Selenium has been shown to protect against several cancers including prostate cancer.

Turkey meat is high in vitamin B3 or niacin, which is needed for metabolism of carbohydrates and for proper nerve function. A 100 g portion of the meat will supply about half of our daily requirement of this vitamin.

Care should be taken in cooking and handling turkey in order to avoid bacterial contamination. Consuming contaminated turkey, especially around Christmas time, is responsible for up to a quarter of all disease outbreaks caused by badly handled food. This is not only due to the bird's size but also because often it has to be cooked well ahead of serving.

In addition, more handling is involved in removing the meat from the carcass, which often has to be done after the meat has cooled down. It has been found that allowing turkey to cool for about three hours at room temperature will give enough time for bacteria to grow and form toxins. The pathogens most likely to be implicated are Clostridium perfringens, Staphylococcus aureus and Salmonella. Since most toxins are resistant to heat, re-heating the meat before serving will not prevent food poisoning. To avoid this problem, once cooked the meat should be kept above 60 or below 7 degrees Celsius. Merry Christmas!

TYPE-2 DIABETES: DIET AND EXERCISE A MUST!

About 20 million North Americans suffer from diabetes, yet almost a quarter of them don't even know it. It is estimated that by the year 2025, a staggering 300 million people worldwide will be suffering from this disease. Although type-2 diabetes affects mostly adults over 40, it has lately been seen in children as well.

Of the two types of diabetes, type-1 is caused by the pancreas not making enough insulin while type-2, which is much more common, is generally the result of the body being unable to use the insulin it makes.

Insulin is needed to bring glucose, which we get from the digestion of carbohydrates, from the blood to our cells so that we can use it for energy. If the glucose stays in the blood rather than being supplied to the cells, we will feel tired due to a lack of energy. In the long run, the build up of glucose in the blood can lead to high blood pressure and heart disease, blurred vision and possibly blindness, kidney problems, recurrent gum infections, and circulation and nerve problems in the feet or legs.

Apart from tiredness, other symptoms include excessive thirst and hunger accompanied by frequent urination as a result of the excess glucose in the blood being removed by the kidneys.

Although there is a genetic component to the disease,

the major factors are age, being overweight, not doing enough exercise and having an unhealthy diet. Smoking increases your risk while drinking three alcoholic drinks per week appears to decrease it. This was the conclusion of the Nurses Study that followed about 85,000 nurses from 1980 to 1996, who were initially free of cancer, heart disease or diabetes. However, the most important factor for predicting diabetes in the group was being overweight.

Fortunately, in the majority of cases, a few lifestyle changes are often enough to reduce the risk of developing the disease.

It has been estimated that compared to someone of healthy weight, the simple fact of being overweight increases the risk of having the disease sevenfold. So, if you do not want diabetes to knock at your door, start to lose weight by increasing your exercise level. According to the Nurses Study and Health Professional Follow-up Study in the US, 30 minutes of brisk walking daily reduced the risk of the disease by 30%.

Exercise combined with a healthy diet works even better. Research carried out at the University of Lund in Sweden showed that through diet and exercise, more than half of early stage type-2 diabetic patients showed no signs of the disease after six years of follow up.

Another study, the Diabetes Prevention Program, has shown that patients who had high blood sugar, but were not yet diabetic, had 58% less cases of diabetes after three years when they lost weight and did more exercise compared to those who did not. In high-risk patients, the simple fact of reducing their weight by only 5-7%, through moderate exercise and diet, could prevent type-2 diabetes.

To better control your blood sugar levels, you should try and keep your carbohydrate consumption to about half of your total calories. Try to avoid the simple carbohydrates that are found in candies and pastries and concentrate instead on the complex ones that are found in whole grains, vegetables, fruits, nuts, peas, lentils and beans. This is because the complex carbohydrates often contain more fibre, which slows down the absorption of glucose from the intestine, thus causing less demand on insulin. In fact, a 2003 paper from the National Public Health Institute of Helsinki, Finland, published in the American Journal of Clinical Nutrition, found that the higher the intake of cereal fibre, the lower the risk of type-2 diabetes.

Research carried out at the University of Texas Southwestern Medical Center in Dallas, and published in May of 2000 in the New England Journal of Medicine, showed that by increasing substantially their intake of fibre to about 15 grams for each of the three meals, type-2 diabetics can effectively reduce their blood sugar level. Two pieces of toast (whole wheat, of course!) with half a cup of baked beans will provide you with that amount of fibre for breakfast.

Foods which contain soluble fibre, such as oat bran, dried beans, peas, apples and most fruits and vegetables, are best for reducing blood sugar levels. If you are at risk of having type-2 diabetes, you should limit consumption of foods with a high glycemic index such as white bread and anything made with refined flour, potatoes, white rice, doughnuts and soft drinks since they will cause the levels of blood sugar and insulin to peak.

Food processing can also influence blood glucose levels. For example, a study at the Bristol Royal Infirmary showed that finely ground wheat or corn was more quickly digested than the corresponding whole or cracked grains, thus resulting in higher blood sugar.

As for protein, choose small portions of lean meat such as chicken or turkey and fish. Since excess protein in the diet is converted to glucose by the liver, an increase in blood glucose level will occur after a few hours of consuming a high protein meal.

The fats in our diet can also have an influence on the development of type-2 diabetes. Saturated fats in meat, butter or cheese and trans fats in margarine and fast foods should be avoided. The good fats are found in olive oil and canola oil but best of all are the omega-3 fatty acids found in fatty fish. According to research carried out in 2002 at Louisiana State University, docosahexaenoic acid, an omega-3 fatty acid found in fatty fish and fish oil, consumed daily over a period of three months improved insulin sensitivity in overweight patients who were at risk of getting diabetes. Scientists recommend a daily intake of 0.6 gram of omega-3 fatty acids, which one can get by eating two fish dinners per week, consisting of fatty fish such as salmon, mackerel, herring or halibut.

There is no sure way to prevent or cure type-2 diabetes, but cinnamon may help. According to research carried out by the US Agricultural Research Unit and published in August 2000, cinnamon increases both the responsiveness of fat cells to insulin and the removal of blood glucose. A polymer found in cinnamon, methyhydroxychalcone polymer, MHCP, is thought to be the active ingredient. One quarter to one teaspoon of cinnamon daily can reduce substantially the risk of type-2 diabetes.

A related cellulose compound, hydroxypropylmethylcellulose, HPMC, when added to fatty food and fed to hamsters slowed down fat absorption and did not increase their risk of getting type-2 diabetes. However, it did not protect them against weight gain!

It appears that drinking a lot of coffee could also protect against type-2 diabetes. Epidemiological studies have found that people drinking 2 cups of coffee or less daily had twice the risk of developing type-2 diabetes compared to those consuming 7 or more cups. This finding applied more to women than men! The study did not distinguish between regular or decaffeinated coffee. Of course, there could be other factors about coffee drinkers that protect them again diabetes.

It is possible that antioxidants such as vitamins C and E as well as the mineral chromium may help but the evidence is not clear-cut.

Since flavonoids are antioxidants, they could help protect against type-2 diabetes by mopping up free radicals which could reduce the effectiveness of insulin action. According to research carried out at the National Public Health Institute of Finland and published in a 2002 issue of the American Journal of Clinical Nutrition, higher intakes of the flavonoids quercetin and myricetin from apples and berries are associated with a reduced risk of type-2 diabetes.

Phytoestrogens, such as isoflavones from soy, may also be beneficial in reducing the risk of diabetes and obesity. Nutritional studies on animals and humans, carried out at USDA Agricultural Research Service in Beltsville and at George Washington University Medical Centre and published in the American Journal of Clinical Nutrition in 2002, indicate that consumption of soy protein and flaxseed is accompanied by better glucose control and improvement in insulin resistance.

In Asia, bitter melon (Mormordica charantia) has long been known to have a hypoglycemic effect. Now a report from the Food and Nutritional Science Program at the University of Hong Kong, and published in 2003 in the Journal of the American Society for Nutritional Sciences, confirmed that when rats are fed a high fat diet supplemented with bitter melon, their serum insulin was lowered, their insulin resistance improved and to top it all, they put on less body fat compared to their counterparts that were fed only the high fat diet.

According to a 2001 article in Diabetes Spectrum, which is published by the American Diabetes Association, in addition to bitter melon, there are several other botanicals such as gymnema, bilberry, garlic and fenugreek that have been used historically to lower blood glucose but there is insufficient clinical data to fully validate their use at present.

Unfortunately, there is no magic bullet for the treatment of type-2 diabetes. However, you can reduce your risk of diabetes by exercising daily, losing weight if you are overweight, and having a heart-healthy diet.

If lifestyle changes are not enough to reduce your blood glucose levels, then anti-diabetic tablets may be prescribed by your physician to aid the pancreas in releasing more insulin and/or to help the body better utilize glucose.

THE IMPORTANCE OF VITAMIN B12

Most people, particularly North Americans, get plenty of vitamin B12 in the foods they eat. That is not always the case, however, for strict vegetarians and for many seniors. The former may not get enough vitamin B12 in their diet while the latter may be unable to absorb the vitamin B12 from the food they eat.

Synthesized by bacteria, vitamin B12 is found mostly in animal foods such as liver, clams, mussels, meat, poultry, fish, milk products and eggs but not in vegetables or fruits. In fact, the richest sources are liver and clams, which have about 40 times the vitamin B12 content of steak. While a 3-ounce portion of steak has 2.1 micrograms, for the same weight mussels have ten times more, crabs four times and salmon just slightly more than that; chicken, turkey or a large egg have about one seventh while a large glass of milk has about half that amount.

It is also available in supplements as cyanocobalamine, which is converted to methylcobalamine and 5-deoxyadenosyl cobalamine, two forms of the vitamin that the body can utilize.

A typical North American diet supplies about 5 to 15 micrograms of vitamin B12 daily, which is more than the daily requirement of about 2 micrograms. However, it is found only in animal foods, so strict vegetarians must take a vitamin B12 supplement in order not to become deficient.

Vitamin B12 is vital for DNA synthesis, the formation of red blood cells and for the health of the nervous system. In addition to vitamin B12, the body also needs iron and folic acid to form red blood cells. A lack of one or more in this trio will produce an insufficient number of red blood cells to carry oxygen throughout the body. This causes anemia, making one tired and prone to infections.

There are two different routes by which vitamin B12 can be absorbed from the intestine. First, foods containing vitamin B12 have to be broken down by stomach acid and enzymes during digestion to free the vitamin. To be absorbed by the intestinal tract, the released vitamin B12 has to combine with a gastric intrinsic factor from the stomach lining, to form a complex, which is then absorbed in the presence of calcium supplied by the pancreas. This results in about 60% of ingested B12 being absorbed.

The other route, by passive diffusion, does not need the intrinsic factor but allows only about 1% of vitamin B12 to be absorbed. Since the body needs only between 1 and 2.5 micrograms per day, supplementation with 100-200 micrograms should be adequate by this route. Calf or lamb liver is so high in vitamin B12 that even people without the intrinsic factor can get enough of it by eating about one pound per day. Admittedly, that's a heck of a lot of liver to eat!

Production of the intrinsic factor, as well as stomach acid, decreases with age resulting in a greater risk of anemia in the elderly. In fact, a study published in the American Journal of Clinical Nutrition in 1994 by researchers at Columbia University, found that 40% of elderly people aged 67 and over suffer from B12 deficiency.

According to the Institute of Medicine of the National Academy of Sciences, people over the age of 50 should get their vitamin B12 from supplements because of poor absorption of this vitamin from animal sources. According to a study at Queen's University, daily supplementation with 25 micrograms of vitamin B12 or eating fortified cereals is enough to prevent a deficiency in most older, healthy people.

For older patients with vitamin B12 deficiency but not suffering from pernicious anemia, research carried out at the Universities of Brussels and Antwerp, and published in the Journal of the American Geriatric Society of 1997, showed that they can be cured after one month's treatment with 100 micrograms per day.

However, for people with pernicious anemia, even higher levels, through injections of 1000 mcg per day, may be needed initially, according to research carried out at the Universities of Washington and Colorado and published in the Journal of American Geriatrics Society in 2002. This high dose is needed to replenish the body stores, following which oral supplementation of lower dosage is prescribed. However, a 1998 paper in the Archives of Neurology showed that oral vitamin B12 replacement is just as effective as B12 injections. Fortunately, vitamin B12 has low toxicity and no adverse reactions have been found when an excess of the vitamin is taken from supplements or food.

Although vitamin B12 is water-soluble, it is not totally excreted when taken in excess but can, in fact, be stored in the body, particularly in the liver and kidney. So, it can take several years, five or more, for the large reserve of vitamin B12 to run out and symptoms of anemia to occur. By the time it appears, the low levels of vitamin B12 could have already caused nerve damage and psychiatric disorders, such as depression, dementia and poor memory. In fact, studies have found that up to 30%

of patients that have been hospitalized because of depression are deficient in vitamin B12.

Although folic acid can cure anemia caused by vitamin B12 deficiency, it will not correct any nerve damage which could become permanent if vitamin B12 supplementation is not started.

Vitamin B12 acts with folic acid and vitamin B6 to control homocysteine levels in the blood. A deficiency of one of these three vitamins can increase blood levels of homocysteine which, in turn, could raise the risk of cardiovascular disease and possibly other diseases such as osteoporosis and Alzheimer's disease. It has been found that taking vitamin B12 and folic acid supplements reduced homocysteine levels in older people and those with vascular disease.

Some elderly patients having symptoms similar to Alzheimer's and a loss of cognitive function have been found to have low blood levels of folate, vitamin B6 and vitamin B12, or high levels of homocysteine. However, a comment in the American Journal of Clinical Nutrition in 2001 pointed out that it is not certain whether the inadequacy of these B vitamins contribute to brain malfunctions or are the result of ageing and disease.

A paper in Canadian Family Medicine in 1997 points out that slightly below normal blood levels of vitamin B12 could be responsible for dementia, hypotension and mood disturbances in people who do not show any sign of anemia.

Long-term use of ulcer medications that suppress acid in the stomach can lead to a deficiency of vitamin B12 in older people according to a 2002 paper in the Journal of the American Geriatrics Society. Similarly, a 2002 paper in the Archives of Internal Medicine found that extended use of anti-diabetes drugs could cause vitamin B12 deficiency. According to a 2000 issue of the same journal, older people suffering from Helicobacter pylori infections can also have a vitamin B12 deficiency.

There are some preliminary indications that a deficiency of vitamin B12 could increase the risk of breast cancer. Researchers at Johns Hopkins University have found that postmenopausal women with the lowest blood level of vitamin B12 had two and a half to four times the risk of getting breast cancer compared to those with the highest levels of the vitamin.

It now appears that blood levels of vitamin B12 may not be a good indicator of the vitamin's level in tissues, which could be low even though blood tests show normal values.

The best test to check for a vitamin B12 deficiency is to measure blood levels of two precursors of metabolic reactions controlled by vitamin B12- homocysteine and methymalonic acid; when levels of these two compounds are high, that of vitamin B12 must be low.

VITAMIN D: THE SUNSHINE NON-VITAMIN!

Strictly speaking, vitamin D is not a vitamin since the body can make it from sunlight; a true vitamin, on the other hand, cannot be made by the body and has to be obtained from the diet. Vitamin D, a fat-soluble vitamin, is now proving to be crucial in protecting the body against bone diseases as well as cancer, heart disease, skin and autoimmune disorders.

For most of us, the major source of vitamin D is through sun exposure, as a result of synthesis of the vitamin by the action of UV rays from the sun on the skin. UVB rays convert a naturally occurring steroid in the skin called 7-dehydrocholesterol to vitamin D. The amount of vitamin D thus formed depends on the season, the time of day, air pollution, the amount of cloud cover and the geographical location in which we live. During the winter months, we get less vitamin D because we stay indoors more and cover more skin with winter clothing. The body then relies on stored vitamin D from the previous summer and what it currently gets from the diet.

One has to be careful though to limit one's exposure to sunshine, as the American Academy of Dermatology points out, so as not to get sunburnt, which could increase the risk of skin cancer. By the way, this risk is accentuated by a high fat diet! For most people, about 15 minutes exposure to sunshine a few times a week should be adequate for vitamin D synthesis.

The recommended adult dose is from 200 to 600 IU per day depending on one's age. Using make-up or sunscreen on the skin, of course, reduces vitamin D formation. To get the same amount of vitamin D, people with darker skin will need longer sun exposure. Dark skin has a higher melanin content and this reduces the formation of vitamin D.

Food sources of vitamin D are not common and include fortified milk, which was first implemented to fight rickets, oily fish such as salmon, sardines and mackerel, cod liver oil and fortified juices, breakfast cereals and margarine. Smaller quantities are found in eggs, beef, butter and vegetable oils. A cup of fortified milk will supply about half the daily requirement of vitamin D for adults up to 50, about a quarter for those 50-70 but only about 15% for those above 70. Cheese, yogurt, ice cream and other milk products do not generally contain any vitamin D.

It is estimated that more than half of the population is not getting an adequate amount of vitamin D due to inadequate exposure to sunlight, low intake from food, lack of absorption from the digestive tract, or inability of the kidney and other organs to convert it to the active form of the vitamin. Infants being breast-fed will lack vitamin D unless the mother or the baby is getting supplements. It is also interesting to note that the ability of the skin to make vitamin D is reduced as we get older, thus increasing the likelihood of vitamin D deficiency.

There are many forms of vitamin D. After it is produced in the skin or obtained from food, vitamin D is first converted to 25-hydroxy vitamin D. It is subsequently transformed to the physiologically active 1, 25-dihydroxy vitamin D mostly in the kidney but also in other organs such as the liver, prostate and the breast. Thus it plays a role not only in bone formation but also in building a healthy immune system and preventing diseases such as cancer and heart disease.

One of the many functions of vitamin D is to promote the absorption of calcium by the body, thus helping to build strong bones. If there is a lack of vitamin D, bones become weak, giving rise to rickets, osteoporosis and osteomalacia. It is estimated that with vitamin D present, 30-50% of calcium in the diet is absorbed but that figure drops to 10-15% when the vitamin is absent. One-third to half of seniors who have suffered hip fractures are thought to have been deficient in vitamin D.

Several studies, including one carried out in Australia and a later one by Swiss researchers, and published in the Journal of the American Geriatrics Society, have shown that supplementation of elderly women with calcium and vitamin D over a period of two years reduced the risk of falls and fractures.

It is not only seniors who are at risk of fractures. Researchers at the University of Otago in New Zealand have found that children three to ten years old who do not drink milk for four months or more have twice the risk of fracturing bones compared to those who do.

Drinking a lot of coffee could result in increased bone loss. A study found that when postmenopausal women consumed more than 300 mg of caffeine (3 cups) per day, they lost more spinal bone mass than those consuming less. However, adding milk to the coffee could minimize this effect.

A recent study carried out by H. Bischoff-Ferrari at the University of Basel and at Harvard Medical School, and published in the Journal of the American Medical Association, on leg weakness, falls and leg fractures in the elderly, found that women who had 800IU of vitamin D daily, together with adequate calcium, had the best protection against falling.

It appears that vitamin D alone can also reduce the risk of

fracture by 22%, as was shown by a 5-year study of 2,500 men over 65 who had one weekly supplementation of the vitamin.

A new form of vitamin D that can grow bone in rats was recently synthesized by H.F. DeLuca at the University of Wisconsin-Madison. If it passes testing in humans, it could become a potential drug for adding bone mass and thus reversing osteoporosis in postmenopausal women.

Mind you, some scientists including Dr. K. McLeod of Binghampton University, regard bone loss in old age as not a disease at all but rather a natural adaptive response to changes occurring in the body!

Recent research on vitamin D indicates that the role of this vitamin in nutrition is not simply to prevent bone loss. By controlling cell growth, energy metabolism and immunity, vitamin D appears to reduce the risk of some deadly diseases such as cancer, multiple sclerosis, rheumatoid arthritis, heart disease and diabetes.

When we increase our exposure to sunlight, more vitamin D is made in the skin, which the liver then transforms into 25-vitamin D. It was previously thought that only the kidneys could subsequently activate the 25-vitamin D into 1,25-vitamin D. However, work by Dr. Michael Holick at Boston University Medical Centre, and others, have shown that 25-vitamin D can also be activated by the colon, breast, prostate and ovaries where it ensures proper cell growth and thus protects against cancer.

For over six decades, researchers have observed a reduced risk of cancer, especially colorectal cancers, with higher intake of calcium and vitamin D, whether from food or from sunlight. In fact, a study of 3,000 mostly men who had undergone a colonoscopy showed that those having the highest vitamin D level had a reduced risk of having a cancerous lesion.

A recent study in the Journal of the American Medical Association confirms that adequate fibre and vitamin D are associated with a lower risk of getting colon polyps, which may lead to colon cancer. In the study involving 3000 men, those who consumed four grams of cereal fibre and 645 IU of vitamin D daily had a reduced risk of colon polyps, while calcium on its own had a much smaller effect.

However, another study in the Journal of the National Cancer Institute reported on a 4-year randomized trial involving 800 people, which showed that both calcium and vitamin D are necessary for the prevention of colon cancer.

Who would have thought that the lack of sunshine, combined with our winter clothing could make a typical Canadian winter somewhat hazardous to one's health? In fact, a report in the Canadian Medical Association Journal, by D. Hanley of the University of Calgary, showed that a whopping 97% of the 188 healthy people aged 27-89 he followed in Calgary had an inadequate vitamin D level, especially during the long dark winter months, thus increasing their risks of osteoporosis and cancer.

Adding further support to the role of vitamin D in this area, a new study of 50,000 men by E. Giovannucci of Harvard School of Public health indicate that higher levels of vitamin D reduced by at least 30% the overall cancer risk.

We all know that the sun increases the risk of skin cancer such as malignant melanoma but could it also be part of the cure? A new study published in the Journal of the National Cancer Institute, by M. Berwick from the University of New Mexico at Albuquerque, found that exposure to the sun may increase one's chances of survival from skin cancer, presumably from the increased vitamin D made in the skin, although early detection could also play a part.

New research from the University of Birmingham and St. George's Hospital in London has shown that the enzyme, which converts vitamin D to its active form, is found not only in the kidney but also in breast tissues. Increasing levels of this enzyme is found in breast tumours which could, in the presence of more vitamin D, prevent its occurrence in the first place. So, women living in northern latitudes may not get enough vitamin D from sunlight, especially in winter, or from the diet to protect them against breast cancer which has, in fact, a lower incidence in sunny Southern Europe. Other factors, such as the low-fat Mediterranean diet, may also play a role.

Scientists at St. George's Hospital Medical School in London are beginning to understand how certain versions of the vitamin D receptor gene, which controls the action of vitamin D in the body, can affect this protective effect. They found that women, who are not predisposed to having breast cancer because they do not have genes such as BRCA1, are twice as likely to have breast cancer when they have particular versions of vitamin D.

In addition to the colon and the breast, the prostate may also be protected by this versatile vitamin. As early as 1998, Holick showed that when 25-vitamin D was added to prostate cancer cells in the laboratory, it was converted to the activated vitamin D, which then ensured a controlled and healthy growth of the cells.

In a later study by H. Li of Harvard University School of Public Health, it was found that men who had higher blood levels of vitamin D had half the risk of developing prostate cancer, especially the most aggressive forms of the disease. Those with higher levels than the median of both 25-hydroxyvitamin D and 1,25- dihydroxyvitamin D had a 45 per cent lower risk of developing aggressive prostate cancer during the 13 years that they were followed.

Rigorous, double blind clinical trials to show whether increasing our vitamin D intake will actually reduce cancer risks have not yet been completed. However, many indications are already pointing in this direction.

It is a fact that the further one lives from the equator, the higher one's blood pressure goes. Could it be that less exposure to sunshine may have an effect on blood pressure and heart disease too? Many medical scientists think so. Of course, other factors such as diet, stress and exercise are involved but lack of vitamin D from sunshine cannot be ruled out. It has even been found that one's blood pressure tends to be lower in the summer than in the winter months!

Many studies have shown that patients with high blood pressure who were exposed to UVB rays in a tanning bed had significant reductions in both diastolic and systolic blood pressures. This was concomitant with an increased blood level of 25-vitamin D. In addition to benefitting patients with hypertension, UVB rays also help those with heart disease attain better heart health, perhaps to the same degree as exercise does.

It is, therefore, not surprising that a group at the University of Bonn reported in the Journal of the American College of Cardiology that blood levels of vitamin D were 50% less in patients with chronic heart failure than in a healthy group. Could vitamin D supplementation help? Well, it appears so since a group led by P.D.Varosy at the University of California at San Francisco found that women over 65 who took 400 IU supplements of vitamin D had a 31 % reduced risk of dying from heart disease compared to those that did not. The use of calcium supplements did not affect the result and the benefits appear to be due to vitamin D alone, which is in fact a regulator for the absorption of calcium by the body.

It is worth noting that atherosclerosis is often accompanied by the accumulation of calcium in the arteries, which some researchers believe is similar to calcification that occurs in bone. Women with osteoporosis have more calcium in their arteries and are more likely to die of heart disease than those with normal bones. However, how this happens is still a mystery!

Why is it that the risk of getting autoimmune diseases such as multiple sclerosis (MS), where the immune system attacks the body, is very much lower near the equator? Could it be due to high levels of vitamin D produced by the strong sun? K.L. Munger of Harvard School of Public Health has produced evidence in the journal Neurology to show the protective effect of vitamin D on MS. She found that women getting 400 IU of vitamin D daily reduced their risk of getting MS by 40% compared to those getting less.

Other groups have found that, in animal studies, administration of 1,25 vitamin D reduces symptoms of other autoimmune diseases including lupus, inflammatory bowel disease and even type-1 diabetes. Since excessive amounts of 1,25-vitamin D can become toxic by dangerously increasing calcium blood levels, synthetic analogues are now available and are being tested in people with autoimmune diseases.

Is it a coincidence that people living in Northern Finland, which gets only a few hours of sunshine a day in winter, have the highest level of type-1 diabetes? Type-1 diabetes is the result of the immune system destroying the cells of the pancreas that produce insulin thus causing a lack of insulin. Finnish babies given vitamin D supplements had an 80% reduction in their risk of getting the disease. Furthermore, a recent study found that a mother's inadequate vitamin D intake while pregnant increases the risk of type-1 diabetes in her offspring.

Although type-2 diabetes is not a disease of the immune

system, vitamin D may have a role in alleviating it too. K. Chiu of the University of California's L.A School of Medicine reported in a paper in The American Journal of Clinical Nutrition that people with low blood levels of vitamin D not only produced less insulin and but also responded less to it.

Since gum disease is the result of inflammation, which is an immune reaction, it is perhaps not surprising to find that, in a survey of 11,200 people, T. Dietrich of Boston University Dental School found that a low blood level of vitamin D could be correlated with gum disease and tooth loss.

In a randomized study of 145 people over 65, scientists working in the Calcium and Bone Metabolism Laboratory at Tufts University also found that those who do not get the recommended daily amounts of calcium and vitamin D were twice as likely to lose teeth compared to those who had adequate amounts. In a similar vein, a study in the same laboratory showed that men and women over 50 with the lowest blood level of vitamin D, had the worst gum conditions and were 25-27% more likely to have tooth loss compared to those with the highest intake.

The risk of getting rheumatoid arthritis, another autoimmune disease, is reduced with vitamin D supplement-ation, according to an article in Arthritis and Rheumatism. Thirty thousand (30,000) postmenopausal women who had a daily intake of 400mg of vitamin D for 11 years reduced their risk of getting rheumatoid arthritis by one third.

Vitamin D supplements could even act as a painkiller in some instances! A study at the University of Minnesota found that 93% of people who complained of recurring, non-specific pain in the arm, back, head and leg were deficient in vitamin D. The aches disappeared with vitamin D supplementation.

Researchers have also found that vitamin D can reduce

SAD or depression during the winter months. This condition is due to the reduction of serotonin as a result of lack of sunshine.

So, if you want to reduce your risk of getting a heart attack and other nasty diseases such as cancer and diabetes, you need to ensure an adequate vitamin D intake from the diet or, preferably, from sunshine. So, don't feel guilty about taking that trip to Florida or Mexico this winter. It may do you good in more ways than one!

NUTRITION FOR SENIORS

The average lifespan in North America has been gradually increasing so that now it stands at 81 years for a female and 76 years for a male. In the next 10 years one in six people will be over 65. Will this increase in longevity be accompanied by better health and less disease?

Fortunately, the risk of getting diseases such as heart disease, cancer, diabetes, obesity and eye diseases can be reduced with better nutrition together with some lifestyle changes. So, eating nutritious and well-balanced meals is important in order to maintain a healthy and active lifestyle. It gives you more energy, makes you more alert and increases your resistance to diseases by building a stronger immune system.

Just like everyone else, seniors need to have a balanced diet consisting of about 60 % carbohydrates, 20% protein and 20% fat. By making wise food choices, you will not only avoid gaining weight as a result of empty calories but also prevent weight loss due to inadequate nutrient intake.

Unfortunately as we get older, our metabolism slows down and calories are used up at a slower rate, which may result in weight gain. In other words, as we get older our calorie needs decrease. In addition, the body may not be able to efficiently extract nutrients from the food we eat.

It is important, therefore, that we eat foods that are nutrient dense so that we get all the protein, fibre, vitamins and minerals we need without excess calories. So, the senior's diet should consist of lots of whole grains, high-fibre cereals, fruits and vegetables, skimmed milk and other low fat dairy products, good sources of protein such as lean white meat, fish, eggs and many plant-based, meat substitutes such as beans, peas, lentils and nuts.

As we get older, we also produce less saliva and stomach acid, which translates into less absorption of vitamins and nutrients from the food we eat. So, we may have to eat more food that contains the nutrients, minerals and vitamins, but without the calories, that we need in order to prevent disease.

For example, more fibre is needed for a healthy digestive system and which will prevent problems such as constipation and diverticulitis. That means eating plenty of whole grains such as whole wheat and multi-grain breads, oats and brown rice which are high in fibre as opposed to white flour products or white rice which, through refining and processing, are almost devoid of their nutrients and fibre.

A high fibre diet will reduce the risk of heart disease, cancer, diabetes and will help keep your weight steady. Soluble fibre present in oats and beans for example, will help flush out the 'bad' cholesterol and so help protect against heart disease. There are also indications that by speeding up transit time in the intestine, insoluble fibre that occurs in grains and vegetables, lowers the risk of colon cancer. Furthermore, foods that are high in fibre are digested slowly and so stabilize blood sugar, which is beneficial to diabetics.

Other good sources of fibre are whole wheat bread, broccoli, carrots, all kinds of beans and nuts, dried figs, prunes, berries, and apples. The peels of fruits and vegetables are also rich in fibre.

Fruits and vegetables of all colours should be consumed liberally since they not only contain minerals, vitamins and fibre that we need but also phytochemicals that are thought to reduce the risk of cancer and other diseases that become more prevalent as we age. Yellow vegetables and fruits are rich in vitamin A. Dark green ones are rich in vitamin A and C, folate, iron, calcium and potassium. Vitamin C is found in citrus fruits, tomatoes, berries, peppers and broccoli. At least, five servings of fruits and vegetables should be consumed daily.

Nuts and beans are not only good sources of protein but also provide many essential minerals such as zinc, magnesium, iron and selenium. Of course, other sources of protein such as fish, meat and eggs should be consumed but the amount of red meat should be limited. These foods will also provide you with much needed vitamin B12.

Seniors should make sure that they consume less sodium in order to reduce their risk of high blood pressure. Instead of adding salt, canned soups or bouillon cubes, flavour foods with spices such as garlic, onions, pepper, oregano and basil.

We should also eat less fat, especially saturated and trans fats, so as to reduce the risk of getting heart disease. Goods fats such as mono and polyunsaturated fats found in olive and canola oils, omega-3 fats found in fatty fish, nuts and seeds should be included as they will help maintain a good cholesterol profile.

Calcium and vitamin D are needed to prevent osteoporosis especially in women. More calcium is needed as we age to maintain bone health. Low fat milk and milk products should be consumed although not butter since it is high in saturated fat. The required daily amount of calcium for seniors is about 1200 mg per day.

By allowing 15 minutes of daily skin exposure to sunlight, you will enable the skin to make all the vitamin D the body needs. Vitamin D can also be obtained from fortified milk or margarine, eggs and fatty fish and is needed to facilitate absorption of calcium by the body to build strong bones.

Post-menopausal women lose more bone mass as a result of the decrease in estrogen while men will experience a similar effect when their testosterone levels drop, usually when they are in their 60's. This bone loss could lead to osteoporosis, which makes bones susceptible to breakage. Good sources of calcium are milk, cheese, yoghurt, broccoli, greens, almonds, tofu, sardines and canned salmon.

We also have to watch our iron levels since most foods contain only small amounts once consumption of red meat has been reduced. Good sources of iron include cereals, dried beans and, of course, red meat. Eating foods that are rich in vitamin C, such as tomatoes or citrus fruits, with meals will increase iron absorption.

Drinking a lot of fluids is also very important since ageing causes faster dehydration. Inadequate fluid consumption will increase the risk of low blood pressure, kidney problems and constipation. To avoid these problems, we need to drink about eight glasses of fluids, which may include water, juices, milk and other beverages.

Free radicals, which can be neutralized by antioxidants, are thought to be involved with many of the diseases of ageing. Pollutants such as smoke, pesticides, ultra-violet radiation and smog are also contributors of free radicals.

When left unchecked, these free radicals can cause damage to the cardiovascular system (by oxidizing LDL cholesterol), to DNA (which can lead to cancer), to the brain (resulting in Parkinson's disease) and to the eye (causing cataracts and macular degeneration).

To reduce free radical damage, avoid exposure to environmental pollutants and eat foods that are rich in antioxidants such as vitamin A, C, and E as well as selenium and zinc.

Ordinarily, you should be able to get all these minerals and vitamins from your food if you are eating properly. So, supplements are not necessary in most cases and will not only be a waste of money but could even be harmful.

As we age, food absorption is reduced partly because the body produces less of the stomach acid that is needed to process food efficiently.

This is especially true of vitamin B12 and, to a smaller extent, folic acid. According to research carried out at Tufts University and published in Nutrition in Clinical Care, one in seven seniors has a deficiency of this vitamin. Low levels of these two vitamins can result in an increase in the blood level of homocysteine, an amino acid that has been linked with cardiovascular disease. Furthermore, as early as 1988, an article in the British Journal of Psychiatry implicated lack of vitamin B12 with an increasing risk of psychotic depression.

Vitamin B12 occurs in meat, eggs, milk and other animal products but not in vegetables or fruits, while folic acid is found in most green vegetables, fruits and grains.

A poor diet combined with a lack of exercise can lead to premature death. One cannot overstate how important regular exercise is. It does not have to be as vigorous as jogging or squash but even brisk walking will help keep you young, healthy and independent. It will also improve your mood and reduce the risk of diseases such as cancer, diabetes and heart disease.

Since weight-bearing exercise have an effect on bone density, walking will result in more minerals being deposited in the bones of the legs, spine and hips thus reducing bone loss. Walking also firms up muscles which will offset the decrease in muscle mass and strength that occurs in ageing. It also increases appetite, which may provide more nutrients.

As we age, we may find it more difficult to prepare food perhaps due to illness or arthritis. In addition, we may lose some of the ability to smell and taste food or maybe even to chew thanks to a loss of teeth. So, if we are in that situation, we need to get help in order to ensure that we continue to get proper nutrition.

Consumption of drugs also increases with age so we have to be on the lookout for possible interaction with food. Grapefruit juice, for example, increases blood levels of drugs such as statins and antihistamines.

Drugs can also interfere with food absorption. Laxatives containing mineral oils can lower absorption of fat-soluble vitamins such as A, D, E and K. Diuretic drugs will increase excretion of water-soluble minerals such as sodium, potassium and magnesium while corticosteroids can inhibit the absorption of calcium.

In summary, we should stay active and eat a wide variety of unprocessed plant-based foods together with some fish and very little red meat. Studies show that people eating a mostly vegetarian diet have less of the diseases associated with ageing.

After all, what is the point in extending our lifespan if we cannot enjoy a good quality of life too?